Remaking Monetary Policy in China

Michael Beggs · Luke Deer

Remaking Monetary Policy in China

Markets and Controls, 1998–2008

palgrave
macmillan

Michael Beggs
Political Economy
University of Sydney
Sydney, NSW, Australia

Luke Deer
Finance
University of Sydney
Sydney, NSW, Australia

ISBN 978-981-13-9725-7 ISBN 978-981-13-9726-4 (eBook)
https://doi.org/10.1007/978-981-13-9726-4

This Palgrave Pivot imprint is published by the registered company Springer Nature Singapore Pte Ltd.
The registered company address is: 152 Beach Road, #21-01/04 Gateway East, Singapore 189721, Singapore

Acknowledgements

Our research has been generously funded by a grant from the Institute for New Economic Thinking.

We have benefitted from conversations with many colleagues and researchers elsewhere. In particular, we would like to thank Chris Jefferis, Chris Aston, Yuxin Yu, and Jackson Mi. We are also grateful for discussions with Daniela Gabor, Jakob Vestergaard, Shaun Breslin, Yang Jiang, and other participants at the China at the Crossroads Conference, 25–26 January 2016, at the Danish Institute for International Studies in Copenhagen, and Beatriz Carillo Garcia, Stephen Bell, Hui Feng, Kellie Tsai, Guonan Ma, and other participants at the Shadow Banking and Alternative Finance in China Workshop, 27 May 2016, hosted by the University of Sydney China Studies Centre.

Finally, this work would not have been possible without the support we have had from Raych and Frankie (Michael) and Rachel and Ziggy (Luke).

Contents

1 **Introduction** 1
References 6

2 **A Bank-Dominated Financial System** 9
2.1 Loans: The Main Source of Finance 10
2.2 Deposits: The Main Financial Asset 12
2.3 Household Assets 13
2.4 Firm Assets 15
2.5 Banking System Structure 16
2.6 Interbank Market 17
References 19

3 **Targets: Why Money and Credit?** 21
References 28

4 **Transmission I: Inside the Banking Black Box** 31
4.1 A Stylised Bank Balance Sheet 32
4.2 The Money Multiplier 35
4.3 The Industrial Organisation Approach 38
References 43

5 Transmission II: Liquidity and Lending 45
5.1 Beyond the Industrial Organisation Approach 47
5.2 Bank Liquidity and Lending 56
Appendix: Note on Figure 5.1 62
References 64

6 Instruments I: Sterilisation and Interest Rate Controls 67
6.1 'Freezing Liquidity': Central Bank Bills and Reserve Requirements 68
6.2 'Dual-Track': Market and Administered Interest Rates 75
References 80

7 Instruments II: The Evolution of Policy Strategy 83
7.1 Influencing the Interbank Market 84
7.2 Last Resort: Window Guidance 91
References 98

8 Conclusion 101
8.1 Summary 102
8.2 Into the 2010s 108
References 112

References 115

Index 123

List of Figures

Fig. 2.1	Aggregate financing to non-financial sector, net new, RMB bn (*Source* PBC/CEIC)	10
Fig. 4.1	Money and bank loan growth year-on-year, per cent (*Source* PBC/CEIC)	34
Fig. 4.2	Depository corporation excess reserves, per cent to deposits (quarterly) (*Source* PBC/CEIC)	38
Fig. 5.1	Change in broad money and its bank sector balance sheet counterparts, RMB bn (quarterly) (*Source* PBC/CEIC, authors' calculations)	50
Fig. 6.1	Change in central bank net assets and bank reserves, year-on-year, RMB bn (*Source* PBC/CEIC, authors' calculations)	70
Fig. 6.2	Selected interest rates (*Source* PBC/CEIC)	77

List of Tables

Table 2.1	Household financial assets (per cent of total)	12
Table 2.2	Household financial uses of funds—flows (RMB bn/% to total)	14
Table 2.3	Non-financial firm financial uses of funds—flows (RMB bn/% to total)	15
Table 2.4	Banking system structure by number and proportion of system assets, December 2005	16
Table 2.5	Interbank market turnover, annual (RMB bn)	18
Table 4.1	Stylised bank balance sheet (with interest rate type)	32
Table 7.1	Money and loan growth: targets and actual; CPI inflation (%)	92

CHAPTER 1

Introduction

Abstract This opening chapter introduces the puzzle the book attempts to solve. The architects of Chinese monetary policy reform in the late 1990s were openly enthusiastic about Western macroeconomics and central banking norms, and proclaimed their intention to abandon credit controls and turn towards market instruments. But by the mid-2000s, policy was relying more heavily on direct bank regulation. Why? We argue that Chinese policymakers departed from Western norms for pragmatic rather than ideological reasons. The 'new macroeconomic consensus' was in fact a normative influence on means as well as aims. But 'normalising' policy was not as easy as simply ditching old for new strategies. The 'normal' instruments of the international macroeconomic consensus depended on financial markets with specific characteristics: (1) a deep money market used by banks and other financial institutions for liquidity management; (2) effective transmission of short-term rates to longer-term rates; and (3) responsiveness of investment to interest rates. These could not be taken for granted in China.

Keywords Monetary policy · China · Liquidity · Central banking · Reform

This book seeks to explain the transformation of Chinese monetary policy in the years before 2008: specifically, why it became *increasingly*

M. Beggs and L. Deer, *Remaking Monetary Policy in China*,
https://doi.org/10.1007/978-981-13-9726-4_1

reliant on direct banking controls in the 2000s in spite of intentions to rely more on market instruments after 1998.

In the mid-2010s, the People's Bank of China (PBC) was announcing moves towards 'market based policy'. A milestone was reached in October 2015 when the PBC removed the ceiling on bank demand and short-term deposit interest rates—the last remaining limit on bank rates. Deputy Governor Yi Gang presented this liberalisation as providing 'basic conditions for transforming the monetary policy framework... facilitating the transition towards price-based instruments' (Yi 2015). Policy would rely more on targeting short- and medium-term interest rates in the interbank market and deregulation of retail rates was necessary to improve transmission out into credit markets. Policy was reaching a 'new normal', which would be more like the West's normal (Deng and Chen 2016; Shevlin 2017; Liu et al. 2017, pp. 1–2; Wang and Mao 2016; Allen et al. 2018, pp. 445–446).

Open market operations had been part of the toolkit in the previous decade, but policy had largely depended on direct controls over commercial banks in tightening policy between 2002 and 2008. Authorities administered deposit and loan interest rates, frequently adjusted reserve requirements, imposed lending limits and issued directives. It would be easy to take a Whig view of the shift to liberalisation: Chinese policy is 'normalising' as authorities shrug off the statist legacy of central planning and move towards an international policy consensus. This fits a familiar story about Chinese economic reform, of tension between ideology and economic rationality: reformers promote rational market-based policy; they are sometimes in the ascendant within the Party and bureaucracy, and sometimes not, but the arc of history bends towards reform.

In this book, we take a different view. The bank-control-based policy framework of the 2000s was not an archaic remnant of planning, but deliberately built in response to financial and macroeconomic conditions, under the influence of the Western 'new macroeconomic consensus'. To understand the transformation of Chinese policy in the 2000s, we need to understand the institutional and market structure of the country's financial system. Chinese policymakers were pragmatic above all. We understand the evolution of their strategy better by looking in some detail at the nature of the system in which they acted.

The notion that policy change has been driven by an ideological shift from 'controls' to 'markets' is misleading. First, the control/market distinction is too blunt. Chinese authorities have tried to increase their reliance on market instruments, primarily because these promised tighter and more flexible policy influence over the financial system.[1] But their effectiveness depended on certain institutional features of interbank markets, which had to be deliberately promoted by the state, as well as the continued and sometimes intensified use of controls. Controls were not an alternative to market-based policy, but an essential condition of them. This is the case in the West as much as in China, but we often take for granted the regulatory structure underpinning 'normal' banking and financial markets.

Second, policymakers could not simply *choose* to rely on market instruments. Flexible and effective open market operations depend on (1) adequately deep interbank markets; and (2) the dependence of banks on those markets for their liquidity management. These are things we often simply assume in discussing monetary policy, but they cannot be assumed in China's case. Interbank markets had to be actively fostered by policymakers in the period we discuss.

We focus on the decade leading up to the turning point of 2008. This period has been overshadowed by what came later: the enormous stimulus in response to the international financial crisis of 2008, the reforms of the 2010s and the reckoning with 'shadow banking'. But the decade between the Asian financial crisis and the global crisis of 2008 is critical to understanding the shape of Chinese monetary policy today.

The 'old normal' Chinese monetary policy framework of the 2000s was *already* the result of a radical transformation under the influence of Western norms. Ideologically, the reforms of the late 1990s involved an enthusiastic adoption of many aspects of international consensus macroeconomic thinking, especially the prioritisation of price stability. But under the macroeconomic conditions of the 2000s, and given the institutional structure of the Chinese financial system, the pursuit of price stability actually led policy to rely *more* heavily on direct bank controls, reversing an earlier intention to abandon credit targets and rely on market-oriented instruments in the interbank market. This was not because

[1] 'Market instruments' can be defined as those instruments involving the transactions (buying, selling, lending, and borrowing) of official agents with other parties who are taking part voluntarily. 'Controls', on the other hand, involve the direction or restriction of other agents. There is no problem analytically distinguishing these instruments while recognising that they are often interdependent in practice. For example, the effectiveness of open market operations in influencing intermediate targets like bank lending may depend on controls such as reserve requirements, as we argue for the case of China.

Chinese policymakers had ideological objections to the international macroeconomic consensus, but because certain features of the Chinese interbank market left it unable to play its role as the main venue of policy. The interbank market was new and underdeveloped, and the central bank had trouble draining a structural surplus of reserves which left the banking system unconstrained by liquidity.

The turn to tighter direct bank controls at mid-decade had a further consequence, which has left a lasting mark on the Chinese financial system: it fed the growth of 'shadow banking' practices which evaded lending controls in various ways. In 2002, bank lending accounted for 95.5% of net new financing to firms and households. By 2008, its share had fallen to 73%.[2] With more financing routing around controls, bank regulation could not remain the lynchpin of policy restraint forever. The outbreak of financial crisis in the United States and Europe in 2008 led Chinese policy to reverse into looseness anyway, leaving this question for the future. But in retrospect, we can see the pre-2008 decade as critical, as controls both helped to foster an interbank market in which policy could be effective, and also promoted the growth of instruments and practices that avoided those controls.

Two norms marked the international 'new consensus' on monetary policy that developed in the 1980s and 1990s (Arestis 2007; Arestis and Sawyer 2008; Bofinger 2001): (1) the proper target of monetary policy is low and stable inflation; and (2) the target should be pursued with market-based instruments, specifically by targeting a key short-term interest rate through open market operations and standing facilities. Chinese policy joined this consensus on *ends*, but departed from it on *means*.

The PBC had once been tasked with a number of goals—including management of the monetary aspects of central planning—but in the course of the 1990s Party and law increasingly committed it to put currency stability first. Inflation in the 1980s had fed the unrest culminating in the debacle in Tiananmen Square (Naughton 2007, pp. 98–99), and a further wave of high inflation in the mid-1990s strengthened the position of those in the bureaucracy pushing for monetary discipline. The 1995 Central Bank Law stated the aim of monetary policy as 'to maintain the stability of the value of currency and thereby promote economic growth'. That put price stability first, as a necessary condition of growth, rather than a goal to pursue alongside growth (Bell and Feng 2013,

[2] Net new 'aggregate financing' data from the PBC/CEIC.

p. 158).[3] The inflationary waves of the 1980s and 1990s had been followed by periods of austerity to bring it under control. Prioritising currency stability set a limit to the pursuit of growth in the short run, in order to promote it over the long run. In 1998 the final abandonment of the Credit Plan, which had subordinated central banking to central planning, signalled that the turn was serious.[4]

But if the new ends of policy were in line with the international consensus, the means were certainly not. Market interest rates were neither the primary policy instrument, nor a major indicative target. The authorities did engage in open market operations, but often with quantity rather than interest rate targets. Instead, policy worked mainly through direct controls on banks: variable reserve requirements, interest rate ceilings and floors, and lending directives. China also set itself apart by remaining committed to a dual target. 'Stability of the value of the currency' meant not just domestic price stability, but also a stable exchange rate—fixed until 2005, then with controlled movement (Allen et al. 2018, pp. 446–448). This left a tension at the heart of the policy regime, since maintaining the exchange rate required the PBC to passively exchange domestic for foreign currency as needed.

Chinese policymakers departed from Western norms for pragmatic rather than ideological reasons. The 'new macroeconomic consensus' was in fact a normative influence on means as well as aims. But 'normalising' policy was not as easy as simply ditching old for new strategies. Dai Xianglong, PBC governor 1995–2002, is said to have distributed to the central bank's staff 100 copies of Mishkin's textbook, *The Economics of Money, Banking and Financial Markets*, a staple of American monetary economics courses. He urged them to consult it regularly and claimed to open it himself every day. The new policy set-up was known as the 'Mishkin framework' (Geiger 2010, p. 1). The difference, officials argued, was not doctrinal but institutional: as one told Bell and Feng (2013, p. 160), 'we are genuine students of Western lectures and doctrines' but 'we came to realise that not all Western doctrines could explain issues in China because of the special and unique situation

[3]As the PBC put it in a 2005 report—suggesting this was still a lesson central bankers felt others needed to hear—'history has proved that oversupply of currency will not bring unchecked acceleration of economic growth, but only price inflation' (PBC 2005, p. 4).

[4]On banking and monetary policy during the transition of the 1980s and 1990s, see Girardin (1997) and Bell and Feng (2013, pp. 155–182). Michell (2012, pp. 154–156) provides a concise overview.

here... We simply don't have the sort of fully-fledged institutions as the advanced economies'.

Even if policymakers saw 'market-based' policy as ultimately desirable, the path was not clear. As PBC Governor Zhou Xiaochuan remarked in 2006, 'if there is a lack of a transmission mechanism, then we cannot rely on those theoretically tempting monetary policies' (quoted in Bell and Feng 2013, p. 160). The 'normal' instruments of the macroeconomic consensus depended on financial markets with specific characteristics: (1) a deep money market used by banks and other financial institutions for liquidity management; (2) effective transmission of short-term rates to longer term rates; and (3) responsiveness of investment to interest rates.

Our aim in this book is to explain what it was about the 'special and unique situation' of the Chinese financial system that made the 'normal' transmission channels unworkable, and how the actual transmission channels were built over the decade to 2008—in particular, why policy came to rely more heavily on direct banking controls. The early years of the new regime were marked by the aftermath of the Asian financial crisis, so that monetary policy remained loose, while the global financial crisis of 2008 was a turning point as policy again switched towards stimulus. We are mainly interested in the problems of restraint in between, in which the transmission mechanism was tested and adapted.

In the next chapter, we describe the basic features of the Chinese financial system in the 2000s and explain why the 'new consensus' transmission channel was unviable. In Chapter 3, we explain why the PBC worked with quantitative money and credit targets, long out of favour in the West. In Chapters 4 and 5, we open the banking 'black box' and explain the logic of the transmission channel through bank balance sheets. In Chapters 6 and 7, we describe how policy met the macroeconomic challenges of the 2000s, and how this drove it to rely increasingly on bank controls and lending directives.

References

Allen, Franklin, Xian Gu, and Jun Qian. 2018. "The People's Bank of China: From 1948 to 2016." In Rodney Edvinsson, Tor Jacobcon, and Daniel Waldenstrom (eds.). *Sveriges Riksbank and the history of central banking*, pp. 418–453. Cambridge: Cambridge University Press.

Arestis, Philip. 2007. "What is the new consensus in macroeconomics?" In Philip Arestis (ed.). *Is there a new consensus in macroeconomics?*, pp. 22–42. London: Palgrave Macmillan.

Arestis, Philip, and Malcolm Sawyer. 2008. "A critical reconsideration of the foundations of monetary policy in the new consensus macroeconomics framework." *Cambridge Journal of Economics* 32 (5), pp. 761–779.

Bell, Stephen, and Hui Feng. 2013. *The rise of the People's Bank of China: The politics of institutional change.* Cambridge, MA: Harvard University Press.

Bofinger, Peter. 2001. *Monetary policy: Goals, institutions, strategies, and instruments.* Oxford: Oxford University Press.

Deng, Haiqing, and Xi Chen. 2016. *Reforging the Central Bank: The top-level design of the Chinese financial system in the new normal.* Singapore: World Scientific Publishing.

Geiger, Michael. 2010. *Monetary policy in China: Institutions, targets, instruments and strategies.* Dissertation, Bayerischen Julius-Maximillians-Universistat Wurzburg.

Girardin, Eric. 1997. *Banking sector reform and credit control in China.* Paris: OECD Development Centre.

Liu, Zheng, Pengfei Wang, and Zhiwei Xu. 2017. "Interest-rate liberalisation and capital misallocations." Federal Reserve Bank of San Francisco Working Paper 2017-15.

Michell, Jo. 2012. *Credit and investment in China: A flow-of-funds analysis.* PhD thesis, SOAS, University of London.

Naughton, Barry. 2007. *The Chinese economy: Transitions and growth.* Cambridge, MA: MIT Press.

People's Bank of China. 2005. *Monetary Policy Report, Quarter 1.* Beijing: People's Bank of China.

Shevlin, Aidan. 2017. "An expanded tool kit for the People's Bank of China." J. P. Morgan. Available at https://blog.jpmorganinstitutional.com/2017/05/expanded-tool-kit-peoples-bank-china. 2 April 2019.

Wang, Gang, and Zhuqing Mao. 2016. "Annual developments in banking regulation." In Bin Hu, Zhentao Yin, and Liansheng Zheng (eds.). *Development of China's financial supervision and regulation*, pp. 59–100. New York: Palgrave Macmillan.

Yi, Gang. 2015. "On the removal of the deposit rate ceiling." Summary of discussion, 27 October 2015. People's Bank of China. Available at http://www.pbc.gov.cn/english/130724/2969444/index.html. 2 April 2019.

CHAPTER 2

A Bank-Dominated Financial System

Abstract This chapter sets the scene for the rest of the book by describing the structure of China's bank-dominated financial system in the 2000s. We focus on six key features: (1) Banks were by far the dominant source of external finance for firms and households. (2) Bank deposits made up most of the financial assets held by households—not just of liquid assets, but of all financial assets. (3) For households, shares were the main alternative financial asset. (4) Non-financial firms accumulated deposits in amounts comparable to households. (5) The banking system was highly concentrated. (6) An interbank market, fostered by authorities, bridged deposit-loan imbalances, and helped banks to manage liquidity.

Keywords Monetary policy · China · Banking · Interbank market · Finance

'In China, the banks are the financial system', write Walter and Howie (2012, p. 27). Banks are at the centre of all financial systems, but in China their dominance goes further. Their deposit liabilities made up not just the bulk of the money supply, but of *all* financial assets held by non-financial units (firms and households). Their lending was not just an important source of external finance, but by far the main source. They were also major players in securities markets. In this chapter, we set the scene by describing the bank-dominated financial structure of the 2000s.

M. Beggs and L. Deer, *Remaking Monetary Policy in China*,
https://doi.org/10.1007/978-981-13-9726-4_2

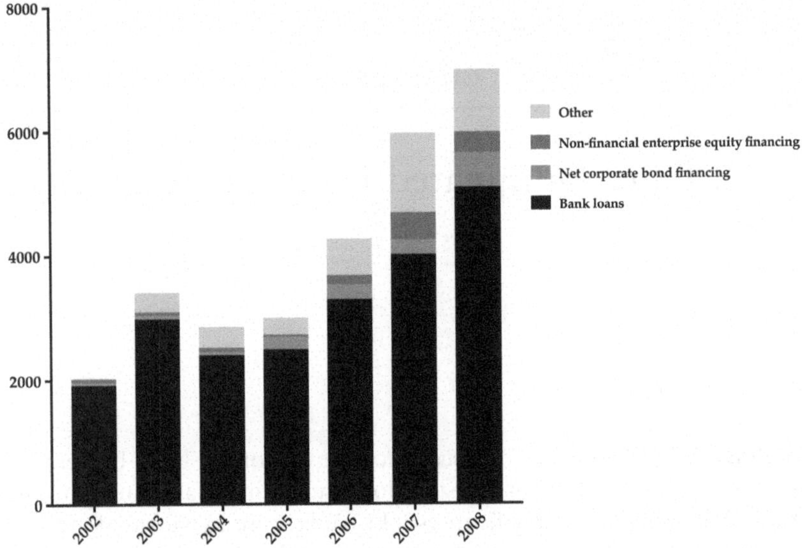

Fig. 2.1 Aggregate financing to non-financial sector, net new, RMB bn (*Source* PBC/CEIC)

2.1 Loans: The Main Source of Finance

Banks were by far the dominant source of external finance for firms and households

Figure 2.1 shows the composition of net new finance extended to the non-financial sector. This is an indicator (sometimes translated as 'total social financing' or 'all-system financing') devised by Chinese authorities in 2011 and calculated as far back as 2002. It reports financing (debt and equity) of enterprises and households, whether extended by intermediaries or by other enterprises and households.[1] The overwhelming

[1] Aggregate financing is unfortunately not a complete measure of the external financing of enterprises and households. It excludes foreign direct investment. It also excludes financing by and to government. Given the blurred boundaries between state and enterprises in China, this calls for caution. For example, local government financing vehicles are counted as enterprises, but local governments themselves are not. When, in 2015, the latter issued a large volume of bonds to repay the debt of the former, aggregate financing stocks declined substantially but somewhat arbitrarily (PBC 2015). But these issues are not important for

importance of bank loans is clear. Securities financing (bonds and shares) made up less than five per cent of new financing in the first half of the decade.

Though bank loans made up most of new financing throughout the period, their share fell from almost complete dominance in 2002 (96%) to just two-thirds by 2007. However, banks were involved in financing beyond bank loans. Most of the 'other' category is made up of entrusted loans and bankers' acceptance bills—forms of inter-enterprise credit that usually involved banks as trustees or guarantors. The bond market was also dominated by banks (Walter and Howie 2012, p. 31); in fact, the main venue for bond trading was known as the 'inter-bank bond market', where more than 90% of outstanding bonds were registered at the end of 2005 (Gao 2007, p. 195). Only 5% were registered on securities exchanges. Commercial banks held more than 70% of bonds, with other financial institutions holding most of the rest (Gao 2007, p. 208; Walter and Howie 2012, p. 31). We must qualify this with the fact that bank holdings were concentrated in *official* bonds of various types—government debt, central bank bills, and the liabilities of the development-financing policy banks. Early in the decade, banks held a negligible proportion of non-financial corporate bonds (the only ones included in the aggregate financing figures represented in Fig. 2.1), but from mid-decade they became substantial holders. (From less than 2% at the beginning of 2005, they held 26% by the beginning of 2008.)[2] Non-financial corporate bonds made up a tiny proportion of all bonds (1.5% by face value of those issued in 2005, and 2.3% of outstanding balances [Gao 2007, p. 193]). So though the banks did not directly dominate financing via corporate bonds, they exerted a major influence on bond pricing as the dominant buyers and holders in the overall market.

the point being made here—that banks dominated the provision of finance in the 2000s. The measure is introduced and described by PBC (2011, pp. 5–6). Both stock (outstanding financing) and flow (net new financing) figures are produced.

[2]Data from China Central Depository & Clearing Co./CEIC series: 'Composition of bond held by investor'.

Table 2.1 Household financial assets (per cent of total)

	Cash	*Deposits*	*Bonds*	*Shares*	*Investment funds*	*Margin trading accounts*	*Insurance technical reserves*
2004	9.9	71.8	3.5	4.9	1.1	0.7	7.8
2005	9.5	72.0	3.1	3.8	1.2	0.7	8.8
2006	8.9	68.3	2.8	6.8	2.2	1.2	9.0
2007	7.5	54.2	2.0	15.4	8.9	3.0	8.1
2008	8.3	66.6	1.5	5.9	5.0	1.4	11.0

Source PBC/CEIC: 'Household financial asset and liability'

2.2 Deposits: The Main Financial Asset

Bank deposits made up most of the financial assets held by households—not just of liquid assets, but of all financial assets.

With banks providing most external financing to the non-financial sector, the other side of the intermediation coin was that bank deposits made up the bulk of financial assets held by non-financial units. We look first at households: Table 2.1 shows the make-up of their aggregate financial asset holdings. Chinese households kept a very large proportion of their financial wealth in deposits: normally more than two-thirds.[3] They also held a large proportion in cash (currency). The 'insurance technical reserve' category includes pension funds—public and private—as well as the reserves of life and other insurance companies, considered in official data as household assets. A remarkable proportion of this category also funnelled into bank deposits: almost 40% of the reserves of both insurance companies (Cao and Ma 2007, p. 236) and the National Social Security Fund (Guo 2007, p. 155) were held in this form. Most of the rest went into bonds—naturally, given their predominance, mainly public rather than corporate bonds.[4] Households held few bonds

[3]For comparison, using figures from the same period, this is much higher not only than in countries with 'market based' financial systems (US: 11.6%; UK: 23.1%; Australia: 17.4%), but also countries with 'bank-centred' financial systems (Germany: 35.2%; Japan: 48.3%). (OECD [2019] figures for 2005. Note these figures include household holdings of currency as well as deposits, but currency holdings are likely to have been minimal.)

[4]In 2004, the National Social Security Fund held 18% of its assets in shares—though some of this too went to the banks, in the form of large equity stakes (Guo 2007, p. 155). By mid-decade, insurance companies were only dipping their toes in the sharemarket,

directly—again mostly government—and they steadily declined as a proportion of financial assets.

2.3 Household Assets

For households, shares were the main alternative financial asset.

Shares were becoming more important—both direct holdings, and via investment funds. Insurance and pension fund accumulation was a steady form of contractual saving, but (wealthy) households moved in and out of the sharemarket more freely. (Real estate also became an important store of value for households—not shown on the table because not a financial asset [Glaeser et al. 2017, pp. 105–106; Cao et al. 2018].) Of course, changes in their share of assets reflect movements in equity prices as well as purchases and sales, but we can track net purchases through flow-of-funds accounts, as shown here in Table 2.2. We see substantial fluctuations in net flows into equities, investment funds, and margin trading accounts. In bearish 2005, for example, households placed a net of just 3.0bn RMB into the stock market directly, 54.6bn RMB into investment funds, and 27.0bn RMB into margin trading deposits. These net flows were minuscule next to net deposit accumulation of 2105.3bn RMB. In bullish 2007, on the other hand, they placed 214.8bn RMB directly into equities, 343.8bn RMB into investment funds, and a mammoth 898.6bn into margin trading deposits. Together these outpaced net deposit acquisition of 1040.7bn RMB.

Household demand for deposits was more responsive to conditions in the sharemarket than to yields on bonds: bondholdings were simply not substantial enough to have much influence. Household liquidity preference largely involved choices among deposits—between demand and saving deposits—and between deposits and shares: direct and via investment funds.

encouraged by officials: In September 2005 less than one per cent of reserves were held in shares directly, but a further 8% went into securities funds (Cao and Ma 2007, p. 236).

Table 2.2 Household financial uses of funds—flows (RMB bn/% to total)

	Currency	*Deposits*	*Bonds*	*Equities*	*Investment funds*	*Margin trading accounts*	*Insurance technical reserves*	*Other*	*Total*
2000	99.4	661.0	69.6	152.7			124.7	−20.4	1087.0
	9%	*61%*	*6%*	*14%*			*11%*	*−2%*	
2001	87.4	997.3	76.4	114.4			115.6	20.7	1411.8
	6%	*71%*	*5%*	*8%*			*8%*	*1%*	
2002	131.9	1425.2	87.9	63.6			254.3	9.2	1972.1
	7%	*72%*	*4%*	*3%*			*13%*	*0%*	
2003	204.8	1656.0	62.6	68.1			303.6	15.9	2311.0
	9%	*72%*	*3%*	*3%*			*13%*	*1%*	
2004	143.4	1567.8	−20.6	71.7			351.6	11.3	2125.3
	7%	*74%*	*−1%*	*3%*			*17%*	*1%*	
2005	212.8	2105.3	24.0	3.0	54.6	27.0	420.2	144.4	2991.3
	7%	*70%*	*1%*	*0%*	*2%*	*1%*	*14%*	*5%*	
2006	252.4	2128.4	41.0	67.2	151.9	341.6	436.5	18.0	3437.0
	7%	*62%*	*1%*	*2%*	*4%*	*10%*	*13%*	*1%*	
2007	274.1	1040.7	−23.6	214.8	343.8	898.6	622.1	139.3	3509.8
	8%	*30%*	*1%*	*6%*	*10%*	*26%*	*18%*	*4%*	
2008	340.2	4677.8	−61.3	287.0	293.6	−534.0	808.4	277.6	6089.3
	6%	*77%*	*−1%*	*5%*	*5%*	*−9%*	*13%*	*5%*	

Source CEIC/PBC

Table 2.3 Non-financial firm financial uses of funds—flows (RMB bn/% to total)

	Currency	*Deposits*	*Settlement funds*	*Bonds*	*Foreign investment*	*Other*	*Total*
2000	10.8	776.6	−369.2	0.0	130.6	448.0	996.7
	1%	*78%*	*−37%*	*0%*	*13%*	*45%*	
2001	9.3	709.6	31.7	0.0	−29.4	86.5	807.7
	1%	*88%*	*4%*	*0%*	*−4%*	*11%*	
2002	14.3	1073.8	5.8	0.0	−36.7	−31.7	1019.7
	1%	*105%*	*1%*	*0%*	*−4%*	*−4%*	
2003	22.2	1577.6	15.2	0.0	−43.7	96.1	1667.3
	1%	*95%*	*1%*	*0%*	*−3%*	*6%*	
2004	15.6	1571.1	−8.5	0.0	18.4	289.8	1886.3
	1%	*83%*	*0%*	*0%*	*1%*	*15%*	
2005	23.0	1247.7	−208.7	0.0	267.0	143.2	1472.2
	2%	*85%*	*−14%*	*0%*	*18%*	*10%*	
2006	27.4	1931.2	169.6	0.0	327.9	353.1	2809.2
	1%	*69%*	*6%*	*0%*	*12%*	*13%*	
2007	29.7	2855.6	50.0	0.0	221.2	367.2	3523.7
	1%	*81%*	*1%*	*0%*	*6%*	*10%*	
2008	37.0	2722.8	0.0	8.7	442.9	547.2	3758.6
	1%	*72%*	*0%*	*0%*	*12%*	*15%*	

Source CEIC/PBC

2.4 Firm Assets

Non-financial firms accumulated deposits in amounts comparable to households.

Households are only part of the story of demand for deposits, however, because firms also held them in large quantities. We do not have balance sheet data for the non-financial enterprise sector, but we do have flow-of-funds accounts. We can see from Table 2.3 that firms (1) accumulated large amounts of financial assets each year—usually not as much as households (except in 2007), but of the same order of magnitude; and (2) accumulated them mainly in the form of deposits. Firms did not acquire bonds or equities, and began placements in investment funds only in small amounts towards the end of our period. (Firm-to-firm lending in the form of entrusted loans and bills makes up part of the 'other' category.)

Table 2.4 Banking system structure by number and proportion of system assets, December 2005

Institution type	*Number*	*Percentage of banking system assets*
Large commercial banks	5	56.1
Shareholding commercial banks	12	11.9
Policy banks	3	7.8
Urban commercial banks	113	5.4
Other domestic banking institutions	27,770	14.1
Foreign banks	173	1.9
Non-bank financial institutions	150	2.7

Source CEIC/PBC

This means the demand for money in China is as much a story of firms as of households. We argue below that much of the demand for deposits was passive in the short run, with important implications for understanding the transmission of monetary policy.

2.5 Banking System Structure

The banking system was highly concentrated.

Table 2.4 shows the number and asset share of each of the main categories of bank, as of December 2005.[5] The largest tier of the system included the 'Big Four' banks separated from the People's Bank of China in the 1980s and commercialised, as well as the largest of the 'shareholding banks', the Bank of Communications.[6] These five banks held more than half the system's assets. In the early and mid-2000s, the 'Big Four' were going through a restructuring process to rationalise bad debt, list them on stock exchanges, and bring in outside shareholders, including

[5]Zeng (2007) provides an overview of the Chinese banking system at mid-decade.

[6]Some sources categorise the Bank of Communications with the 'large state-owned banks' on account of its size, and some with the 'shareholding banks', due to its legal designation. The public listings of the 'Big Four', and injections of private capital, blurred the boundaries between them and the 'shareholding banks', while state-owned entities owned much of the Bank of Communications's stock. We include it in the former category because that is where official statistics now include it. In December 2005, the month of the data in Table 2.4, it held 3.6% of total banking system assets, making it much smaller than the average 'large commercial bank' but much bigger than the average 'shareholding commercial bank'.

international banks, but they remained majority-owned by the state. The next group was comprised of the 12 ‘shareholding banks’ (other than the Bank of Communications), owned by groups of firms and private investors, with some listed on exchanges. These were small only in comparison to the giants above, and as a group were growing more quickly. The ‘policy banks’ are a category apart: really branches of government dedicated to financing state projects. They fund themselves with bonds rather than deposits—but their assets are counted as part of the banking system’s in official statistics. Beyond this concentrated core of banks with a national scope were hundreds of smaller urban banks and tens of thousands of local small-scale rural banks and credit cooperatives, as well as the assorted branches of many foreign banks.[7] The ‘non-bank financial institutions’ category here includes bank-like intermediaries such as trust and finance companies, but not insurance companies or funds. They had an important future, but were still a very small part of the system at this stage.

2.6 Interbank Market

An interbank market, fostered by authorities, bridged deposit-loan imbalances and helped banks to manage liquidity.

In China, informal interbank markets can be traced back to the early 1980s, but they were regulated only in the 1990s (Geiger 2010, pp. 11–13). The PBC’s first attempt at open market operations that decade had been abandoned because of their chaotic impact on bank liquidity in the absence of a well-organised market. This led authorities to organise a formal interbank market, launched in 1997 (Bell and Feng 2013, p. 170), with a mandatory electronic trading system so that activity took place in full view of the PBC. The central bank had powers to licence participants and regulate allowable terms and other characteristics of the instruments traded.

The structure of the banking system shaped the pattern of the interbank market. Deposit rate ceilings largely prevented banks from competing for deposits, but a mismatch between lending and deposit market shares meant some banks depended on borrowing reserves from others: the medium-sized shareholding banks tended to be net interbank

[7] Also, at the fringes and statistically invisible, a substantial informal banking system (Tsai 2002).

Table 2.5 Interbank market turnover, annual (RMB bn)

	Interbank loans	*Repo*	*Spot bond*	*Commercial bills*	*Central bank bills*	*Short-term financing bonds*
1997	414.9	32.0	1.0	274.0	0.0	
1998	98.9	105.5	3.3	240.0	0.0	
1999	329.2	403.4	7.7	244.9	0.0	
2000	668.9	1636.8	68.2	644.7	0.0	
2001	781.3	4022.3	80.9	1269.9	0.0	
2002	1210.7	10,580.0	431.9	2310.2	0.0	
2003	2411.3	14,703.3	3038.5	4539.4	943.9	
2004	1441.9	11,768.8	2513.4	4705.7	1147.1	
2005	1278.3	21,628.4	5953.7	6750.8	3066.3	
2006	2150.3	36,507.3	10,205.2	5430.0[a]	4568.6	
2007	10,646.6	59,688.4	15,621.2	5870.0[a]	9207.6	
2008	15,049.2	93,526.1	37,143.2	7100.0[a]	25,147.3	253.1

Source National Interbank Funding Center/CEIC, PBC/CEIC, China Central Depository & Clearing Co. (chinabond.com.cn), Yin (2007, p. 162)
[a]Note that there is a break in the commercial bills data from 2006. We take data from Yin (2007) for 1997–2005. After that series ends we rely on PBC/CEIC data, which is available from 2004. This data is clearly less precise and there are large differences between them and Yin's numbers where the sources overlap. (PBC/CEIC reports 3400 bn RMB for 2004 and 4450 bn RMB for 2005.)

borrowers; the large state-owned banks, where deposits concentrated, net interbank lenders (Yin 2007, pp. 164, 168; Walter and Howie 2012, pp. 32–33).

Table 2.5 shows the turnover of different instruments on the interbank market. Initially the system mainly encompassed interbank loans and commercial bill trading, but authorities successfully encouraged interbank bond trading to shift there from the public exchanges—and, as mentioned above, most bonds were held by banks, so this became the main bond market. Banks typically held bonds to maturity, making them little different from loans in some respects (Walter and Howie 2012, pp. 102–112). But they were used as collateral in repurchase agreements, which became the dominant form of trading on the market, with unsecured interbank borrowing mainly limited to the larger banks.

Traditionally most interbank borrowing in China was longer term—for fundraising, not liquidity management. In 1997, at the outset of the new system, more than half of interbank borrowing (unsecured and via repurchase agreements (or 'repos')) was for terms of at least

30 days (Li and Peng 2002, p. 8). Turnover quickly fell away to negligible levels between 1998 and 2000—the Asian financial crisis depressing demand for credit and leaving banks flush with reserves (see Table 2.5). Authorities had to actively foster the market and encourage its use for liquidity management, and this project continued through the period we are looking at. By the time the market resurged in 2000, the short end had come to predominate: two-third of interbank loans and repos had terms of seven days or less (Geiger 2010, p. 13; Li and Peng 2002, p. 8)—a striking shift.

From there the market continued to grow (though dropping back temporarily from a 2003 peak as foreign exchange sterilisation flooded banks with reserves [Yin 2007, pp. 165–166, 171]). But it was still not ready to bear the weight of policy—as we discuss below.

References

Bell, Stephen, and Hui Feng. 2013. *The rise of the People's Bank of China: The politics of institutional change.* Cambridge, MA: Harvard University Press.

Cao, Honghui, and Mengmeng Ma. 2007. "The stock exchange market." In Yang Li (ed.). *China's banking & financial markets: The internal research report of the Chinese government*, pp. 223–248. Singapore: Wiley.

Cao, Yujin, Jidong Chen, and Qinghua Zhang. 2018. "Housing investment in Urban China." *Journal of Comparative Economics* 46, pp. 212–247.

Gao, Zhanjun. 2007. "The inter-bank bond market." In Yang Li (ed.). *China's banking & financial markets: The internal research report of the Chinese government*, pp. 191–222. Singapore: Wiley.

Geiger, Michael. 2010. *Monetary policy in China: Institutions, targets, instruments and strategies.* Dissertation, Bayerischen Julius-Maximillians-Universistat Wurzburg.

Glaeser, Edward, Wei Huang, Yueran Ma, and Andrei Shleifer. 2017. "A real estate boom with Chinese characteristics." *Journal of Economic Perspectives* 31 (1), pp. 93–116.

Guo, Xiaoting. 2007. "The securities industry." In Yang Li (ed.). *China's banking & financial markets: The internal research report of the Chinese government*, pp. 133–158. Singapore: Wiley.

Li, Yang, and Xingyun Peng. 2002. "The money market in China: Theory and practice." *China & World Economy* 3, pp. 3–10.

OECD. 2019. "Household financial assets (indicator)." Available at https://doi.org/10.1787/7519b9dc-en. 3 April 2019.

People's Bank of China. 2011. *Monetary Policy Report, Quarter 1.* Beijing: People's Bank of China.

People's Bank of China. 2015. *Monetary Policy Report, Quarter 3.* Beijing: People's Bank of China.

Tsai, Kellee S. 2002. *Back-Alley banking: Private entrepreneurs in China*. Ithaca, NY: Cornell University Press.

Walter, Carl E., and Fraser J. T. Howie. 2012. *Red capitalism: The fragile financial foundation of China's extraordinary rise*, 2nd ed. Singapore: Wiley.

Yin, Jianfeng. 2007. "The banking industry." In Yang Li (ed.). *China's banking & financial markets: The internal research report of the Chinese government*, pp. 161–190. Singapore: Wiley.

Zeng, Gang. 2007. "The banking industry." In Yang Li (ed.). *China's banking & financial markets: The internal research report of the Chinese government*, pp. 69–95. Singapore: Wiley.

CHAPTER 3

Targets: Why Money and Credit?

Abstract The People's Bank of China was not very explicit about its views on the transmission processes of monetary policy in the 2000s, but its statements were oriented around money and credit quantity targets. This contrasted with international 'new macroeconomic consensus' policy, which focused on interest rates. We explain why Chinese officials continued to use quantitative targets: mainly as an anchor for tighter policy, rather than any belief in a stable demand-for-money function. Interest rates were not appropriate as an intermediate target because policymakers doubted their influence on investment.

Keywords Monetary policy · China · Central banking · Money · Credit · Targets

The PBC was not very explicit about its views on the transmission processes of monetary policy, but its statements were oriented around a pair of quantitative targets: growth in the money supply, and growth in bank credit, with M2 the key monetary aggregate, which includes cash and all commercial bank deposits.[1] This contrasted with international 'new

[1] The PBC had begun announcing M1 and M2 targets in 1994 as it began winding down the Credit Plan (Bell and Feng 2013, pp. 165–167), and decided on M2 as the key aggregate in 1996. It continued to announce M2 targets through the 2000s, but dropped M1 in 2007 (Sun 2013, p. 59).

M. Beggs and L. Deer, *Remaking Monetary Policy in China*,
https://doi.org/10.1007/978-981-13-9726-4_3

macroeconomic consensus' policy, which focused on interest rates. In this section we explain why Chinese officials continued to use quantitative targets: mainly as an anchor for tighter policy, rather than any belief in a stable demand-for-money function. (The targets set each year can be found in Table 7.1, in Chapter 7, where we discuss policy strategy in pursuing them.)

Policymakers doubted the influence of interest rates on investment and demand more broadly. As a PBC official bluntly put it, 'the effects of interest rate cuts on saving deposits, consumption, bank loans, and investment growth are all insignificant… the interest rate is unqualified to be a target of monetary policy operations' (Xie 2004, p. 28, and see evidence, pp. 22–25). Research throughout the decade continued to cast doubt on the macroeconomic impact of interest rate changes (Mehrotra 2007; Laurens and Maino 2007). Koivu (2009, p. 464) finds the link to be strengthening but 'still weak'.

There are a number of reasons why this may have been so. First, we should not exaggerate the unusualness of this finding: Studies in the UK and United States have long found no strong relationship between interest rates and corporate investment, perhaps because of the confounding influence of difficult-to-measure shifts in expected profits and general confidence (Chick 1983, pp. 129–131; Kothari et al. 2014). Second, state-owned firms—abundant in China—may have been insensitive to interest rates because they have only a 'soft budget constraint' (Xie 2004, p. 24) and are not motivated by strict economic rationality. But private investment was also insensitive to interest rates. It may be, third, that firms were indifferent to modest shifts in interest rates because of a very high average rate of return on investment—above 15%, compared with the 5–10% normal elsewhere (Bai et al. 2006). Finally, many firms had large flows of retained funds, which accumulated into large stocks of bank deposits; they could make large investments without needing to borrow.

But if Chinese policymakers doubted the effectiveness of interest rate targeting, policymakers elsewhere were sceptical about quantitative monetary targeting. Monetary targeting depends on both the predictability of the demand for money and on authorities' ability to control supply. In the West, the monetary targeting experiments of the 1970s and 1980s had been abandoned after running into problems on both fronts, and quantitative targets played little to no role in the policy of the 2000s (Goodhart 2007; Blinder 1998, pp. 26–29).

It is difficult to believe the PBC was unaware of the theoretical and practical problems of monetary targeting.[2] So why were quantitative targets seemingly central to Chinese policy? Michell (2012, p. 176) argues that 'the apparent similarity of the Chinese regime to episodes in advanced economies during which policy was guided by monetarist doctrine is misleading', because Chinese policymakers did not assume a stable money multiplier relationship between the monetary base and broader aggregates. We agree that they did not believe in the simple textbook monetarist models. Central bankers recognised their imperfect control of the base, the variability of the money multiplier (M2/base ratio), and the instability of the demand-for-money function. The main purpose of the targets was as a clear anchor for tighter policy—especially a *political* anchor—and this did not depend on a belief in the stability of demand or on the precise predictability of supply.

At least early on, however, there was at least some belief in textbook monetarism, along with ambiguity and debate. Looking back from the 2010s, former PBC and CBRC officials Yan and Li (2016, p. 192) state in no uncertain terms that 'money is endogenous in the economy and uncontrollable by the central bank', i.e., the central bank did not have the power to set the money supply directly because it was mainly made up of commercial bank deposits, which did not respond mechanically to central bank instruments. But Yan and Li (2016, p. 192) also claim that 'the primary cause of the weak transmission mechanism in China is the fact that currency is taken as an exogenous variable controlled by the central bank'. In other words, other policymakers had not always shared their view.

[2]The Mishkin textbook Dai promoted at the PBC introduces monetary policy through the control of the monetary base and the bank money multiplier, and the demand-for-money function. But it is presented explicitly as an over-simple model used for pedagogical purposes. Mishkin (1995, pp. 379–380, 383–402) acknowledges that variability in the money multiplier means that the central bank does not necessarily control the money supply even if it controls the monetary base. He also makes clear that the stability of demand for money in the United States seemed to break down after the mid-1970s and that the Federal Reserve abandoned monetary targets by the early 1990s (Mishkin 1995, p. 511). He describes the simple monetarist model of the transmission process of monetary policy as a 'black box', depending on statistical regularities between money supply and aggregate nominal income but not explaining the channel of cause and effect (Mishkin 1995, p. 657). (We refer to the edition most likely to have been originally distributed by Dai at the PBC, but these passages remain in later editions.)

In the 1990s and 2000s several studies estimated money demand functions for China. Most claimed to find stability in the function—surprisingly, given a background of radical institutional change—but they differed widely in their estimates of the coefficients. Chen (1997, p. 610) regretted that the differences were large enough to make it hard for policymakers to draw practical conclusions: for example, Hafer and Kutan's (1994) estimates called for M2 growth below 28.5%, while Huang's (1994) called for 34%. Chen (1997, p. 610) himself called for further study.

But later studies continued the pattern: Each claimed to find a stable function relating the growth of a monetary aggregate and income over the long run, but with quite different estimates of the coefficients, and different conclusions about the importance—and even direction of effect—of other variables such as interest rates and stock prices (Bahmani-Oskooee and Wang 2007; Mehrotra 2008; Wu 2009; Baharumshah et al. 2009). Zuo and Park (2011) survey the studies and suggest that the differences reflect the fact that the various estimates have samples covering different time periods, while the evolution of the financial system continually changed the relationship: the money demand function had in fact *not* been stable.

Furthermore, the studies found relationships between money and income only over the long run, not tight relationships that held continuously. As Gerlach and Kong (2005) put it, a 'money overhang'—the difference between the *observed* monetary stock and *estimated* demand for money—may be a leading indicator of future inflation, but actual stocks of money could be out of equilibrium with demand for years. 'The response of inflation to money shocks is gradual and peaks at about 20 quarters' (Gerlach and Kong 2005, p. 13). Similarly, Burdekin and Siklos (2008, pp. 856–857) estimate a 'money gap' and note a slower response of inflation to the gap in the 2000s than in the 1990s.

If the underlying demand-for-money function was changing over time, and if it held only over the long run anyway, estimates would be highly uncertain and not seem a promising guide for policy. But fine-tuning was not the point of the monetary targets for the PBC, which acknowledged that the income velocity of money (and so its inverse, demand for money) was not stable, due to factors including 'the situation of financial technology, interest rate, degree of economic stability or confidence... inflation expectation and income level' (PBC 2005, pp. 4–5). It made a pragmatic and cautious use of monetary aggregates as a general indicator of liquidity. Households and firms seemed prepared to hold large money balances relative to income or revenue for long periods of time, but a build-up in liquidity meant *potential* for inflation, which was reason enough to keep it under control.

Perhaps the most important point of the quantity targets was to *politically* legitimate monetary restraint. This is clearest when we turn to consider the other side of monetary targeting—the controllability of the money supply. Official quantity targets were indeed *targets* rather than policy settings. Money could escape policy control due either to:

- variability in the money multiplier—the ratio between the monetary base and the target money aggregate—if banks did not keep to a regular reserve-deposit ratio and/or if the public varied its demand for cash holdings; or
- lack of control of the monetary base, either because the central bank accommodated bank demand for reserves or was unwilling or unable to fully sterilise the impact of its foreign exchange purchases.

Officials and economists recognised that factors beyond policy control were involved in determining the money supply,[3] but used this as an argument for restructuring the financial system to strengthen policy control. Yu and Xie (1999, p. 43) argued that the monetary base was 'rather endogenous' because 'political, institutional, and technical barricades prevent the PBC from enforcing satisfactory control'. This was not meant as an argument against monetary targeting, but in favour of removing those barricades so the targets could be more effectively pursued. Taking liquidity control seriously called for changes across a range of economic policy. Growth targets would need to take them into account. The government should no longer expect the central bank to fund public deficits directly. Banks should be transformed into more commercially oriented entities, and their bad loans dealt with so solvency concerns would not force the central bank to indiscriminately provide a liquidity backstop. The exchange rate would need to become more

[3]A 2003 PBC report explained that hitting the monetary targets could be difficult because of time lags in the transmission process, and because the bank money multiplier varied (PBC 2003, Box 1).

flexible, because under a fixed rate international payments imbalances affected the monetary base (Yu and Xie 1999, pp. 36–37).[4]

This, ultimately, was the primary function of monetary targets for Chinese policy: as an anchor for discipline. They were not only an internal operational guide for the bank, but a way of coordinating with other branches of policy, and of providing an easily communicable rationale for central bank restraint. Policymakers recognised their imperfect control of the base, the variability of the money multiplier, and the instability of the demand-for-money function. The targets were pursued, as we will see, with a variety of bank controls and other devices, including 'moral suasion' and influence over borrowing by state-owned enterprises (Michell 2012, p. 176). But this had been the case in the advanced economies also: monetary targeting in the West had also been unable to rely on control of the base, or a stable monetary multiplier, and had relied on bank controls.[5] In the West, too, the main function of targets had been as an anchor for tighter policy, political as much as economic.[6]

What about the bank credit target? At first, the monetary targets were often presented as an *alternative* to controls over bank credit (Bell and Feng 2013, pp. 163–165). Credit quotas were associated with the old Credit Plan, where they had been used for ambitious growth targets rather than macroeconomic restraint, and the central bank had often lacked the power to enforce limits on the banks (Yu and Xie 1999, pp. 34–35; Xiong 2012, p. 515). The monetary targets were thought to bring a discipline the credit plan had lacked. But in fact money and credit targets were not alternatives, and policy came to focus increasingly on the latter for two reasons. First, the aggregates are not independent variables. They are linked through bank balance sheets, as we discuss below. Bank loans create deposits, so that control over the monetary targets

[4]As discussed below, the authorities would deal with the monetary effects of the large balance-of-payments surpluses of the 2000s with various sterilisation methods. The currency was also allowed to appreciate later in the decade.

[5]Goodhart (1989, pp. 357–377) discusses this for the case of the United Kingdom, and Beggs (2015, pp. 230–243) for Australia.

[6]Blinder (1998, p. 29) describes the US Federal Reserve's turn to monetarism 1979–1982 as a political 'marriage of convenience' rather than an economic conversion: 'Monetarist rhetoric provided the Fed with a political heat shield as it raised interest rates to excruciating heights'.

runs through bank credit. Second, credit is a direct influence on expenditure in its own right.

Within the 'new macroeconomic consensus' internationally, credit was coming to be recognised as a potentially important part of the transmission channel of monetary policy. Though policy practice had by the late 1990s converged to a standard framework based on adjusting the interbank interest rate, there was much theoretical uncertainty about how the transmission process worked. Central bankers often claimed to be agnostic: in 1999, Otmas Issing, chief economist of the European Central Bank, wrote, 'we can only safely say that we know, at best, the broad contours of the euro-area transmission mechanism right now', while Deputy Governor of the Bank of England Mervyn King said that at least in the short run, 'the effect of monetary policy is neither sufficiently well understood nor sufficiently stable over time' (both quoted in Bofinger 2001, p. 72). Alan Blinder (1998, pp. 26–29), former Vice-Chairman of the Federal Reserve, explained that empirical and practical considerations, more than theory, led policy to target interest rates rather than monetary aggregates. The Mishkin textbook so influential at the PBC describes the monetarist transmission mechanism as a 'black box whose workings cannot be seen' (Mishkin 1995, p. 657). But this was true also of the interest rate channel. Confidence in the use of interest rates to guide output back towards potential was based on a view that it worked in practice, not a definite view of *how* it worked.

But as we have seen, Chinese policymakers did *not* believe interest rate-based policy would work practically, and so had to pay more attention to other channels of transmission. In Western academic debates, the idea of a 'credit channel' had gained ground in the 1990s: Bernanke, Blinder, Gertler, and others argued that the macroeconomic effects of monetary policy were too rapid, too strong and too sustained to be fully explained by traditional interest rate channels—that is, via opportunity cost and the cost of capital. They proposed that effects were also running through balance sheet effects on banks, firms, and households (Bernanke and Blinder 1992; Bernanke and Gertler 1995). They focused attention on the effects of policy on the financing of expenditure and the supply of and demand for credit. The availability and cost of bank financing matters because many businesses and most households do not have direct access to market financing, and so are dependent on banks or bank-like institutions for their borrowing (Bernanke and Gertler 1995, p. 40).

If this was true in a relatively market-based financial system like that of the United States, it was much truer in China, where bank loans were the source of more than 90% of external finance to firms and households in the early 2000s. There is no doubt Chinese authorities were aware of the literature. The Mishkin textbook beloved by Governor Dai reviewed it (Mishkin 1995, pp. 631–632), and two of the transmission mechanisms the textbook discusses run through bank loans (Mishkin 1995, pp. 672–674).[7] A later edition of Mishkin's text suggests that the bank lending channel may have been more of historical than current relevance for the American economy, because deregulation had given banks there more recourse to money market fundraising to get around reserve constraints (Mishkin 2004, p. 622). But in China, not only was the interbank market less developed, but authorities retained direct controls over bank lending. It is no wonder the bank lending channel seemed important to Chinese policymakers.

References

Baharumshah, Ahmad Zubaidi, Siti Hamizah Mohd, and Marial Awou Yol. 2009. "Stock prices and demand for money in China: New evidence." *Journal of International Financial Markets, Institutions and Money* 19, pp. 171–187.

Bahmani-Oskooee, Mohsen, and Yongqing Wang. 2007. "How stable is the demand for money in China?" *Journal of Economic Development* 32, pp. 21–33.

Bai, Chong-En, Chang-Tai Hsieh, and Yingyi Qian. 2006. "The return to capital in China." NBER Working Paper Series 12755.

Beggs, Michael. 2015. *Inflation and the making of Australian macroeconomic policy, 1945–85*. Houndmills: Palgrave Macmillan.

Bell, Stephen, and Hui Feng. 2013. *The rise of the People's Bank of China: The politics of institutional change*. Cambridge, MA: Harvard University Press.

Bernanke, Ben S., and Alan S. Blinder. 1992. "The Federal funds rate and the channels of monetary transmission." *American Economic Review* 82 (4), pp. 901–921.

Bernanke, Ben S., and Mark Gertler. 1995. "Inside the black box: The credit channel of monetary policy transmission." *Journal of Economic Perspectives* 9 (4), pp. 27–48.

[7] In later versions of the textbook, *four* of the nine transmission channels discussed run through bank loans (Mishkin 2004, p. 619).

Blinder, Alan S. 1998. *Central banking in theory and practice.* Cambridge, MA: MIT Press.

Bofinger, Peter. 2001. *Monetary policy: Goals, institutions, strategies, and instruments.* Oxford: Oxford University Press.

Burdekin, Richard C. K., and Pierre L. Siklos. 2008. "What has driven Chinese monetary policy since 1990? Investigating the People's Bank's policy rule." *Journal of International Money and Finance* 27, pp. 847–859.

Chen, Baizhu. 1997. "Long-run money demand and inflation in China." *Journal of Macroeconomics* 19 (3), pp. 609–617.

Chick, Victoria. 1983. *Macroeconomics after Keynes: A reconsideration of the general theory.* Cambridge: MIT Press.

Gerlach, Stefan, and Janet Kong. 2005. "Money and inflation in China." Hong Kong Monetary Authority Research Memorandum 04/2005.

Goodhart, Charles A. E. 1989. *Money, information, and uncertainty.* Houndmills: Macmillan.

Goodhart, Charles A. E. 2007. "Whatever became of the monetary aggregates?" *National Institute Economic Review* 200, pp. 56–61.

Hafer, Rik W., and Ali M. Kutan. 1994. "Economic reforms and long-run money demand in China: Implications for monetary policy." *Southern Economic Journal* 60 (4), pp. 936–945.

Huang, Guobo. 1994. "Money demand in China in the reform period: An error correction model." *Applied Economics* 26, pp. 713–719.

Koivu, Tuuli. 2009. "Has the Chinese economy become more sensitive to interest rates? Studying credit demand in China." *China Economic Review* 20 (3), pp. 455–470.

Kothari, S. P., Jonathan Lewellen, and Jerold B. Warner. 2014. "The behaviour of aggregate corporate investment." MIT Sloan School Working Papers 5112-14.

Laurens, Bernard J., and Rodolfo Maino. 2007. "China: Strengthening monetary policy implementation." IMF Working Paper 07/14.

Mehrotra, Aaron. 2007. "Exchange and interest rate channels during a deflationary era: Evidence from Japan, Hong Kong and China." *Journal of Comparative Economics* 35 (1), pp. 188–210.

Mehrotra, Aaron. 2008. "Demand for money in transition: Evidence from China's disinflation." *International Advances in Economic Research* 14, pp. 36–47.

Michell, Jo. 2012. *Credit and investment in China: A flow-of-funds analysis.* PhD thesis, SOAS, University of London.

Mishkin, Frederic S. 1995. *Economics of money, banking, and financial markets,* 4th ed. New York: HarperCollins.

Mishkin, Frederic S. 2004. *Economics of money, banking, and financial markets,* 7th ed. Boston: Addison Wesley.

People's Bank of China. 2003. *Monetary Policy Report, Quarter 4.* Beijing: People's Bank of China.

People's Bank of China. 2005. *Monetary Policy Report, Quarter 1.* Beijing: People's Bank of China.

Sun, Rongrong. 2013. "Does monetary policy matter in China? A narrative approach." *China Economic Review* 26, pp. 56–74.

Wu, Ge. 2009. "Broad money demand and asset substitution in China." IMF Working Paper 09/131.

Xie, Ping. 2004. "China's monetary policy: 1998–2002." Stanford Center for International Development Working Paper 217.

Xiong, Weibo. 2012. "Measuring the monetary policy stance of the People's Bank of China: An ordered probit analysis." *China Economic Review* 23 (3), pp. 512–533.

Yan, Qingmin, and Jianhua Li. 2016. *Regulating China's shadow banks.* Milton Park: Routledge.

Yu, Qiao, and Ping Xie. 1999. "Money aggregates management: Problems and prospects in China's economic transition." *Contemporary Economic Policy* 17 (1), pp. 33–43.

Zuo, Haomiao, and Sung Y. Park. 2011. "Money demand in China and time-varying cointegration." *China Economic Journal* 22 (3), pp. 330–343.

CHAPTER 4

Transmission I: Inside the Banking Black Box

Abstract This is the first of a pair of chapters opening the 'black box' of the banking system to understand the transmission mechanism through which the People's Bank of China tried to influence its money and credit intermediate target variables. Here we discuss two unsatisfactory visions of the process: the simple bank money multiplier approach, and the 'industrial organisation' framework treating banks as intermediaries of 'funds' between depositors and borrowers. Chinese policymakers rejected both of these ways of looking at policy transmission through banks.

Keywords Monetary policy · China · Transmission · Money multiplier · Industrial organisation

In this chapter and the next we open the 'black box' of the banking system to understand the transmission mechanism through which the PBC tried to influence its money and credit intermediate target variables. This requires some imaginative reconstruction, because the PBC did not publicly present an official view of the transmission mechanism. We noted in the last chapter that 'new consensus' theory did not have a settled view on the matter. Here we first discuss two unsatisfactory visions of the process: the simple bank money multiplier approach, and the 'industrial organisation' framework treating banks as intermediaries for 'funds' between depositors and borrowers. We show that Chinese

M. Beggs and L. Deer, *Remaking Monetary Policy in China*,
https://doi.org/10.1007/978-981-13-9726-4_4

Table 4.1 Stylised bank balance sheet (with interest rate type)

Assets	*Liabilities*
Loans (***benchmarked rates***)	Deposits (***administered rates***)
Bonds/bills (***market rates***)	
Interbank loans/reverse repos (***market rates***)	Interbank borrowing/repos (***market rates***)
Excess reserves (***administered rate***)	
Required reserves (***administered rate***)	
	(Capital)

policymakers rejected them. In Chapter 5 we then present an alternative vision, focused on bank liquidity preference and the supply and demand for reserves in the interbank market. This is consistent with the framework outlined by Sun (2015), a policy 'frontbencher' at the PBC, in various papers from the period. We show that it resembles a 'money view' understanding of central banking as the management of liquidity in the interbank money market. This framework helps us to understand what Chinese policymakers were trying to do, and the obstacles that led them to rely ultimately on direct restraint of bank lending.

4.1 A Stylised Bank Balance Sheet

The central bank's targets were related to one another through the balance sheet of the banking sector: loans are the largest component of bank assets, and most of the money supply is made up of deposits, the largest component of bank liabilities. To understand the relationship between the targets, and to explore the policy transmission mechanisms, it is helpful to work with a stylised bank balance sheet, as shown in Table 4.1.

Most of these categories are made up of an assortment of different assets/liabilities, and could be further subdivided by term, risk, etc. Accordingly, each category has a structure of interest rates rather than a single rate. (For example, there is no single deposit rate, but a rate for demand deposits, 3-month term deposits, 1-year term deposits, and so on.) But the structures within each category tended to move together, so it is not simplifying too much to speak of a representative 'loan rate', 'deposit rate', etc.

The interrelation between rates on different categories of asset is important in understanding the banks' position linking the interbank money market and the longer-term credit market. The balance sheet indicates whether the rates of each instrument class were administered, benchmark, or market rates. In China's 'dual-track' interest rate regime (He and Wang 2012), the authorities regulated bank lending and deposit rates, while letting other rates be determined on the market. Specifically, authorities set benchmarks as well as maxima and minima for deposit and loan rates at each term. (Rates paid on bank reserves were simply set by the central bank.) We consider loan rates as 'benchmarked' rather than administered, because in 2004 the loan rate ceiling was removed, and actual loan rates were generally above the floor and so in principle free to move around at banks' discretion (Geiger 2010, pp. 73–74). Though riskier loans could be priced as high as twice the benchmark, the whole structure tended to move when authorities moved the benchmark—so though it was not compulsory, the benchmark gave policymakers substantial control over actual loan rates (Chen et al. 2017, p. 5). Though the deposit rate *floor* was removed at the same time as the loan rate ceiling, actual deposit rates pushed up against the ceiling—the equilibrium rate was apparently higher—making for tighter control over deposit rates.

The stylised balance sheet can represent the whole banking sector, or an individual bank. In the aggregate balance sheet for the banking sector, interbank loans and borrowing largely cancel out, leaving some net lending on the asset side, since banks in the aggregate were a net lender to non-bank financial institutions.[1]

Rates of growth of bank credit and of *M2* were close for much of the decade, as can be seen in Fig. 4.1.[2] Since the two sides of the balance

[1] Note that an individual bank may be both a lender and a borrower on the interbank market: For example, it may have lent longer term, but needed to borrow at a shorter maturity to cover a reserve shortfall. Note also that when we discuss 'banks' here, unless otherwise stated we include the range of institutions counted as 'other depository institutions' in official Chinese statistics (i.e., 'other' than the PBC itself), which includes bank-like institutions such as rural credit cooperatives.

[2] Both *M2* and the volume of bank loans have exponential growth trends, so must be detrended for a meaningful measure of their relationship. We took natural logarithms of both variables to linearise the trends. We then obtained detrended variables by regressing each on time (months since beginning of the series) and taking the residuals. The R-squared for the relationship between (log) *M2* residuals and (log) loan residuals over the whole period January 1997–December 2008 is 0.52. This indicates that variation in

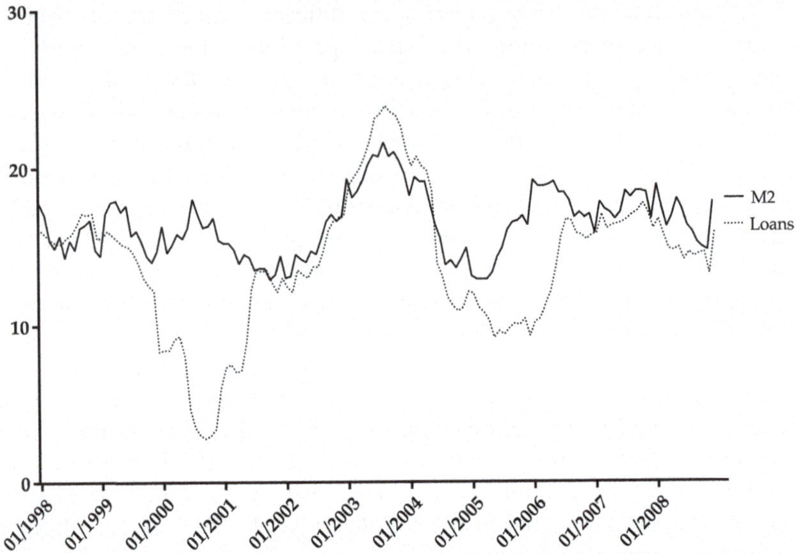

Fig. 4.1 Money and bank loan growth year-on-year, per cent (*Source* PBC/CEIC)

sheet must match, this is not surprising, given the predominance of deposits within the money supply and the predominance of loans among bank assets. It is the two periods where money and loan growth diverge that call for explanation. The first, from mid-1999 to mid-2001, was the deflationary aftermath of the Asian financial crisis. Loans grew slowly while banks added disproportionately to their stocks of government bonds, other financial institution bonds (probably largely policy bank bonds), and foreign assets.[3] The second, at mid-decade, involved the

loans around its trend accounts for about half of the variation in *M2* around its trend. The relationship is much tighter for the sub-period July 2001–December 2008, i.e., after the period of abnormally low loan growth associated with the aftermath of the Asian crisis. For this sub-period, R-squared is 0.75.

[3]These three categories together—in roughly equal proportions—account for most of the difference between the growth in deposits and the growth in loans in the year to March 2001. On the liability side, there is also a sizeable decline in bank borrowing from the central bank. Bank balance sheet data is patchy before 2002, and there are two more series changes in official statistics between then and 2008, so we have not attempted to

sterilisation of foreign exchange inflow on a large scale: much of the gap between deposit and loan growth is accounted for by bank accumulation of reserves and central bank bonds—an episode we discuss in Chapter 6.[4] Other factors were longer-running trends: increasing bank holdings of government bonds, the restructuring of non-performing loans, and the shift of the non-bank public from cash to deposits (PBC 2005, pp. 4–7).

4.2 The Money Multiplier

The link between loan and money growth brings us to the critical question for understanding the transmission mechanism: causation. What drove the pace of growth of these two variables, and what are the potential levers of policy influence? We first discuss two unsatisfactory answers, and then in the next chapter develop our answer in contrast to these. The first approach is the money multiplier, which focuses on the ratios between the monetary base, money, and bank credit. If these ratios are constant or predictable, and if the authorities control the monetary base, they thereby control money and credit. This is still familiar from textbooks though it is now usually presented as a simplistic starting point rather than how things really work[5]—which is also how we shall treat it. The constancy of money and credit multipliers depends on very restrictive assumptions.

construct a table or chart representing balance sheets for the whole period. We draw this PBC data from the CEIC China Premium database Table CN.KC, 'Deposit money bank' assets and liabilities. We focus on the year to March 2001, because later that year there is a large change in the unidentified 'Net other item' category, representing a discrepancy between recorded assets and liabilities. This probably corresponds to items added in the next series beginning in 2002, including foreign currency deposits, interbank assets/liabilities, and 'other assets'.

[4] For data to the end of 2005 refer again here to the 'Deposit money bank' assets and liabilities series in CEIC Table CN.KC. Figures in this period are more complete than for before 2002, but again by the end of 2005 discrepancies are accumulating, and the 'Deposit money bank' series ends there. From there the 'Other depository corporation' series begins ('Other' here means 'other than the central bank').

[5] The textbook Governor Dai distributed at the PBC is typical in this respect, first setting out the multiplier and then explaining that 'the actual creation of deposits is much less mechanical than the simple model indicates' (Mishkin 1995, p. 379, and see pp. 367–433).

The money supply ($M2$) is comprised of bank deposits and currency in the hands of households and non-bank firms. The monetary base is made up of bank reserves and currency. The ratio of money supply to monetary base would be constant only in a simple world where (1) banks keep a constant reserve-deposit ratio, and (2) the public keeps to a constant currency-deposit ratio.[6] There would also be a constant ratio between the money supply and bank credit only if, in addition, banks held no assets but loans and reserves, or stuck to a constant ratio of non-loan assets to loans.[7] In other words, the money and credit multipliers depend upon bank balance sheets passively adjusting to changes in reserves. It would be enough for policy control purposes—assuming, for the sake of argument, that the central bank can and wants to control the monetary base—for these ratios to be predictable rather than constant.

In fact, only the currency-deposit ratio (non-bank holdings of cash relative to deposits) was relatively predictable. It declined over the 2000s, falling by more than half from 15.6% to below 7%, as the public continued to shift its money holdings from cash to deposits (Yong 2011, p. 23).[8] This change was a steady trend (with a regular seasonal spike

[6]The money multiplier relationship is derived as follows: If $M2$ is the monetary aggregate of interest, including currency and all deposits, and MB is the monetary base, then the money multiplier is the ratio of $M2$ to MB ($m = M2/MB$). $M2$ is made of currency in the hands of the public (C) and deposits (D) ($M2 = C + D$). The monetary base is made up of currency in the hands of the public (C) and reserves (R) (including currency held by the banks and bank deposits with the central bank) ($MB = C + R$). Let k be the currency-deposit ratio ($k = C/D$). Let r be the bank reserve-deposit ratio ($r = R/D$). Then $m = (C+D)/(C+R) = (k+1)/(k+r)$. If both k and r are constants, so will be m. If either or both vary, so will m.

[7]In this case, the bank balance sheet identity means that the sum of loans (L) and reserves (R) must equal deposits (D) ($L + R = D$). Since we assume banks maintain a stable reserve-deposit ratio (r), $L = D - rD = (1 - r)D$. Since $M2 = C + D$, and $C = kD$ (see previous footnote), $D = M2/(1+k)$. Therefore, $L = M2 \times (1-r)/(1+k)$. Aggregate bank credit has a constant relationship to the money supply, and since the money supply has a constant relationship to the monetary base, so does credit. Specifically, the ratio of loans to the monetary base, or loan multiplier ($l = L/MB$), is $(1-r)/(k+r)$. An $M2$ target implies a credit target, and vice versa, with both having constant ratios to the monetary base. (If banks hold assets besides loans and reserves, this opens up another potential wedge in the loan-reserve and loan-deposit ratios, and to maintain a constant multiplier we also need to assume a constant ratio of non-loan assets to loans in order to maintain a constant relationship between loans and deposits.)

[8]Depositors also tended over the decade to shift a larger proportion of their money holdings from demand deposits to longer term deposits, so that the $M1/M2$ ratio declined by 8.2% between 1999 and 2010 (Yong 2011, p. 39).

each New Year). But the banks did not keep to a constant reserve-deposit ratio either—and in this case, variation was less predictable. Because the PBC varied the required reserve ratio, nobody would expect a fixed relationship between *all* reserves and bank deposits—the question is whether banks gravitated towards a constant or predictable ratio of *excess* reserves to deposits. As can be seen in Fig. 4.2, the answer is no: the banking system[9] held considerable excess reserves, and the ratio could fluctuate substantially. There was a seasonal element in excess reserve fluctuations, and a general downward trend, but not a smooth one. Banks were not 'fully loaned up'. Thus the ratio of *M2* to monetary base could shift a great deal, both because of the variable reserve requirements, and also because the banks had leeway to vary their excess reserves (Sun 2015 [1995], p. 40).[10] As for credit, we have already noted that banks did not always maintain a fixed ratio of loans to deposits: The make-up of their asset portfolios shifted in the proportions allocated to securities, loans, and reserves.

Chinese policymakers could not, then, believe in a stable money multiplier. As one put it, it may be an 'effective teaching tool' but is 'not realistic' (Sun 2015 [1995], 35).[11] There is no reason to expect the ratios to remain stable because they 'actually are balanced results of many asset demand functions and supply functions of the central bank, banks and the nonbank private sector' (pp. 39–40). If the determinants of supply and demand change, the ratios will change. It may be useful to track the relationship between bank reserves and deposits—as an indicator of bank liquidity—but the analyst should treat the money multiplier equation as an identity rather than explanatory in itself. In any case 'the monetary base cannot be completely controlled by the monetary authority' (p. 39), and policymakers often attempted to control the price of borrowing reserves rather than their quantity.

[9] Included here are all deposit-taking institutions, which were all covered by the required reserve ratio—urban and rural credit unions, financial companies, investment trustee companies, and financial leasing companies as well as commercial banks. Commercial banks were by far the largest category, however.

[10] In other words, k followed a generally steady downward trend, but r fluctuated in a less predictable way.

[11] Sun's (2015) book collects past papers written by the PBC economist, mostly unpublished. We have indicated in square brackets the year in which each paper was originally written.

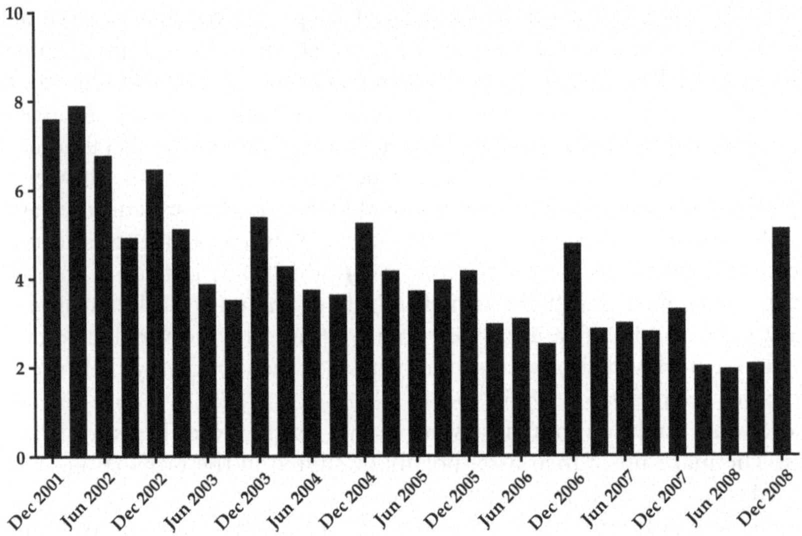

Fig. 4.2 Depository corporation excess reserves, per cent to deposits (quarterly) (*Source* PBC/CEIC)

4.3 The Industrial Organisation Approach

If the relationship between reserves, deposits, and loans was a matter of, as Sun put it, 'many asset demand functions and supply functions of the central bank, banks and the nonbank private sector' (Sun 2015 [1995], pp. 39–40), what was the nature of those functions, and how did they interact? The 'industrial organisation' framework (Freixas and Rochet 2008, pp. 69–126) is one popular alternative to the money multiplier approach, and representative of modern microeconomic approaches to bank behaviour. It has been adapted in a number of studies of China's financial system (Feyzioglu et al. 2009; Porter and Xu 2009, 2016; He and Wang 2012; Chen et al. 2013). Freixas and Rochet (2008, p. 72) present the framework as an alternative to the 'simplistic' multiplier approach, which errs in treating banks as 'passive entities'. Instead, banks are modelled as managing their balance sheets to maximise profit.

Each bank's revenue is the interest earned on its assets; its costs include the interest paid on its liabilities plus the cost of administering loans and deposits. In the absence of regulatory barriers, a bank expands its balance sheet to the point where the expected marginal revenue from assets equals marginal cost. Banks also manage the composition of their balance sheets to maximise profit: They allocate assets between loans, money market lending and reserves, and liabilities between deposits and money market borrowing. A profit maximisation equation for each bank determines:

- Its supply schedule for funds in the loans market, relating its supply of loans to the difference between the loan interest rate and the money market rate.[12] Banks have an incentive to lend to firms/households until the marginal revenue from loans (adjusted for risk), less the money market interest rate, equals the marginal administrative cost of loans.
- Its demand schedule for funds in the deposit market. Symmetrically, a bank is willing to borrow in the form of deposits rather than on the money market so long as the spread covers the marginal cost of administering deposits—taking into account the fact that some proportion of deposits must be held as less-remunerative required reserves.
- Its net lending to the money market, which may be positive or negative. Since the balance sheet must balance, this is equal to the bank's deposits, minus its loans and reserves. (The model abstracts from bank capital.)

Banks are treated as intermediaries between a loan market on which they supply funds, and a deposit market on which they demand funds. On both markets, they interact with non-bank firms and households. Individual bank loan supply schedules sum together to find the market loan supply schedule, which meets a firm/household loan demand schedule. The demand for loans is presumed to be negatively related to the loan rate. Likewise, the bank deposit demand schedules sum to a sector demand schedule, which meets the firm/household deposit supply

[12] If there are economies of scope between the management of loans and deposits (e.g., if information gathered from deposits reduces the cost of information gathering for lending purposes), the deposit rate will also affect the supply of loans and the loan rate will affect bank demand for deposited funds (Freixas and Rochet 2008, pp. 73–75). The Chinese models generally abstract from such economies of scope, which complicate exposition of the model without much practical importance.

schedule. The supply of funds for deposit is presumed to be positively related to the deposit rate.

Finally, the interbank market must also clear. The fact that each bank's balance sheet must balance means that the determination of its loans and deposits also determines the amount it lends to or borrows from the interbank market (taking into account that some ratio to deposits must be held in the form of required reserves). Without participation by the central bank or non-bank financial institutions, the supply of lending banks must be equal to demand for borrowing banks. Together this determines the market-clearing loan, deposit, and interbank rates, and the quantity of loans and deposits.

Monetary policy can be brought into the model by introducing the central bank as a participant in the money market. In the basic model, without central bank intervention, interest rates and the quantity of loans and deposits depend ultimately on firm and household preferences, given the cost structure and state of competition in the banking sector. (The model was originally designed to focus attention on this last feature—thus the 'industrial organisation' approach.) Banks are simply intermediaries, and they set loan and deposit rates above and below the money market rate so that marginal revenue equals the marginal cost of administering loans and deposits. The money market rate itself adjusts to clear that market, and so ultimately brings household/firm desired borrowing in line with desired deposit-holding. But if the central bank intervenes in the money market, it can achieve any target interest rate by supplying or withdrawing funds. The lending and deposit rates will follow the money market, and given the household/firm demand and supply schedules, this will determine the quantities of loans and deposits.

The Chinese studies have adapted the industrial organisation model in various ways to reflect the institutional features of the Chinese financial system. Here we focus on the models of He and Wang (2012) and Porter and Xu (2016):

1. *Bank security holdings*: Banks hold securities, mainly Treasury bonds and central bank bills. These are treated as substitutes for interbank loans, so that their yield is equal to the money market rate (again, note that both rates stand in for a structure of rates reflecting term and risk) (He and Wang 2012, pp. 931–934; Porter and Xu 2016, pp. 151–53). In Freixas and Rochet (2008), households hold bonds but banks do not; the Chinese studies

reverse the assumption, since in China most bonds are held by banks.[13] This adaptation has little impact on the model, but it allows it to deal with a point of central bank intervention of some importance in China: the issuance of central bank bills. Both Freixas and Rochet (2008) and the Chinese studies abstract from securities as an alternative source of finance for firms—a fairly realistic abstraction in China, where bonds and equities are a minor source, at least early in the 2000s (see Fig. 2.1).

2. *Regulated bank interest rates*: The models of both He and Wang (2012, p. 935) and Porter and Xu (2016, pp. 148, 153–154) treat the deposit rate as constrained by the regulatory ceiling, but the loan rate as unconstrained by the floor. Nevertheless, Porter and Xu (2016, p. 154) treat the loan rate as an administered rather than market rate, arguing that the loan market does not clear and the loan rate in practice follows the benchmark, being relatively unresponsive to demand. He and Wang (2012, p. 935), on the other hand, view the loan rate as market-clearing: though credit quotas may make the loan supply curve vertical at the point of maximum allowable lending, banks raise rates to clear the market at that quantity.[14] We believe Porter and Xu's (2016) assumption is more realistic: banks rationed funds while loan pricing tended to take the benchmark loan rate as its basis. This is in line with historical experience from other countries, that administrative lending quotas have led banks to ration funds at customary rates rather than raise rates, 'over a wide range of examples' (Goodhart 1989: 158).
3. *'Window guidance' and credit quotas*: The PBC has the power to give banks directives about both the sectoral composition and the overall quantity of their lending. These can range from advice and moral suasion to binding quotas. The details are not published

[13]At the end of 2005, commercial banks held 70.7% of outstanding bonds, while personal investors and non-financial investors held just 0.6% and 0.2%, respectively. Households held bonds indirectly via funds (4.2%), while insurance companies held 6.7%. Most of the rest were held by non-bank financial institutions (4.5%), credit unions (2.4%), and by 'special settlement members' (4.9%) and securities exchanges (5.4%) (Gao 2007, p. 208).

[14]There is more discussion on this point in an earlier version of the paper (He and Wang 2011, pp. 13–15).

and so there is much uncertainty about the nature and force of the 'guidance', but there is general agreement that monetary policy leaned more heavily on direct lending controls as the decade progressed, as we discuss in Chapter 7. This can be incorporated into the model as a constraint in the profit maximisation problem, potentially holding the volume of loans below equilibrium (He and Wang 2011, pp. 13–15; Porter and Xu 2016, pp. 151–53).

4. *High levels of excess reserves*: In the Freixas and Rochet model, banks do not hold reserves beyond the level mandated by reserve requirements. So long as reserves are remunerated at a rate below the money market rate, no profit maximising bank would hold more than they had to, under the model's assumptions. But in 2000s China, banks in the aggregate held reserves well above the required ratio to deposits, as can be seen in Fig. 4.2. He and Wang (2012) do not include excess reserves in their model, but Porter and Xu (2016, pp. 151–153) do, as we discuss in Sect. 5.2.

The Chinese studies use the industrial organisation framework to ask different questions from what it was initially designed for. For Freixas and Rochet (2008), the model answers the question of how central bank intervention in the money market works through profit-maximising bank balance sheet management to determine lending and deposit volumes and interest rates (and the impact of structures of competition in the banking system). The Chinese adaptations acknowledge that policymakers directly administered bank interest rates and controlled lending volumes with window guidance. The original question is irrelevant in these conditions: the Chinese bank did not rely upon money market intervention to reach its target variables. These studies are concerned with something different: the determination of money market interest rates *given* bank rate controls.[15]

Our own question is different again: we are seeking to understand why Chinese policy relied upon interest rate and direct lending controls in the first place. The adaptations of the Friexas-Rochet approach move it towards realism regarding Chinese conditions. But if a financial system works the way it does in the basic Freixas-Rochet model, it is not clear why Chinese policy would rely on such controls. Open market

[15] Feyzioglu et al. (2009) tackle the related question of what would happen to the interest rate structure if bank rates were liberalised.

operations would be enough to control the interbank interest rate, which is the marginal cost of funds to banks. Given bank profit maximisation and the structure of competition, this would be sufficient to control lending rates, and given non-bank preferences, the volume of loans. Policy would simply need to respond to shifts in the non-banks' demand schedule for loans and supply schedule for deposits as necessary to meet its targets.

The industrial organisation approach has fundamental problems that make it unsuited to answering this question. It rightly treats banks as strategic actors, unlike the simple money multiplier. But it misleadingly considers them simply as channels for 'funds' from depositors to borrowers, failing to recognise the active role of bank lending in determining the quantity of deposits as well as loans. It misses the importance of liquidity management to bank behaviour, and of liquidity as a basic constraint on bank expansion. Finally, it assumes that banks always adapt their balance sheets to maximise profit, when in reality Chinese banks seem to have allowed buffer stocks of reserves to adjust passively at least in the short run, due to uncertainty and/or costs involved with active reserve management. We develop these points in the next chapter.

References

Chen, Hongyi, Qianying Chen, and Stefan Gerlach. 2013. "The implementation of monetary policy in China: The interbank market and bank lending." In Bang Nam Jeon and María Pía Olivero (eds.). *Global banking, financial markets and crises*, pp. 31–69. Bingley: Emerald Group Publishing.

Chen, Hongyi, Michael Funke, Ivan Lozev, and Andrew Tsang. 2017. "To guide or not to guide? Quantitative monetary policy tools and macroeconomic dynamics in China." Bank of Finland Institute for Economies in Transition Discussion Papers 3.

Feyzioglu, Tarhan, Nathan Porter, and Elod Takats. 2009. "Interest rate liberalisation in China." IMF Working Papers 09/171.

Freixas, Xavier, and Jean-Charles Rochet. 2008. *Microeconomics of banking*. Cambridge, MA: MIT Press.

Gao, Zhanjun. 2007. "The inter-bank bond market." In Yang Li (ed.). *China's banking & financial markets: The internal research report of the Chinese government*, pp. 191–222. Singapore: Wiley.

Geiger, Michael. 2010. *Monetary policy in China: Institutions, targets, instruments and strategies.* Dissertation, Bayerischen Julius-Maximillians-Universistat Wurzburg.

Goodhart, Charles A. E. 1989. *Money, information, and uncertainty.* Houndmills: Macmillan.

He, Dong, and Honglin Wang. 2011. "Dual-track interest rates and the conduct of monetary policy in China." Hong Kong Institute for Monetary Research Working Paper 21.

He, Dong, and Honglin Wang. 2012. "Dual-track interest rates and the conduct of monetary policy in China." *China Economic Review* 23, pp. 928–947.

Mishkin, Frederic S. 1995. *Economics of money, banking, and financial markets*, 4th ed. New York: HarperCollins.

People's Bank of China. 2005. *Monetary Policy Report, Quarter 4.* Beijing: People's Bank of China.

Porter, Nathan, and TengTeng Xu. 2009. "What drives China's interbank market?" IMF Working Paper 09/189.

Porter, Nathan, and TengTeng Xu. 2016. "Money-market rates and retail interest regulation in China: The disconnect between interbank and retail credit conditions." *International Journal of Central Banking* 12 (1), pp. 143–198.

Sun, Guofeng. 2015. *Reforms in China's monetary policy: A frontbencher's perspective.* New York: Palgrave Macmillan.

Yong, Cao. 2011. "The persistence of strong money supply growth in China: The forces of endogenous determinants." *Banks and Bank Systems* 6 (4), pp. 33–48.

CHAPTER 5

Transmission II: Liquidity and Lending

Abstract This is the second of a pair of chapters opening the 'black box' of the banking system to understand the transmission mechanism through which the People's Bank of China tried to influence its money and credit intermediate target variables. Here we present a critique of the 'industrial organisation' framework and develop an alternative that fits with Chinese policymakers' statements. Banks in the aggregate are not constrained by a need to raise deposits, but by the cost and availability of liquidity in the form of reserves. We discuss how this manifested in the Chinese financial system—not so much to explain how policy was able to use the bank liquidity constraint to manage lending, but to show why this was difficult in the 2000s.

Keywords Monetary policy · China · Liquidity · Central banking · Lending · Credit

In a paper originally published in China in 2001, PBC monetary policy 'frontbencher' Sun Guofeng (2015 [2001]) sharply criticised models of money and banking that treat banks as intermediaries for 'funds' between depositors and borrowers. The implication that banks are constrained by a need to first raise 'funds' in order to lend is misleading.

M. Beggs and L. Deer, *Remaking Monetary Policy in China*,
https://doi.org/10.1007/978-981-13-9726-4_5

> [I]n the conventional money theory, there is a concept of 'fund' that can be held by both banks and clients. This fund exists only in people's minds, similar to the 'ether' in physics... Banks' lending activity is in itself a self-balancing behaviour of the double-entry bookkeeping. When clients receive loans from a bank, their deposits in the bank will increase at the same time. Banks' credit (i.e., deposit liabilities) is accepted by the public, so banks can create deposit money by lending... Deposits do not constrain lending activities; the only constraint on lending activities is the requirement to hold reserves.... (Sun 2015 [2001], p. 18)

The industrial organisation framework is open to Sun's objection. Freixas and Rochet (2008) do not refer to generic 'funds' but do treat deposits as something demanded by banks and supplied by households. The 'supply' of deposits depends only on the deposit interest rate, the implication being that this rate must increase if the volume of deposits is to increase: they must be attracted from households. At the same time, the approach neglects the liquidity constraint on bank expansion: liquidity is unimportant in the model and banks hold only just enough reserves to meet an arbitrary reserve requirement. Such a framework does not represent how Chinese policymakers saw the banking system. Our argument is relevant to any banking system, but the problems are perhaps easier to overlook when policy works through the transmission of money market rates to longer term rates—quantities can be neglected with less consequence.[1] But in China, where policy transmission via interest rates was unreliable, it is more important to understand the relationship between quantities of credit and money, as well as the logic of causation. In this chapter, we develop such an understanding—not so much to explain how policy was able to use the bank liquidity constraint to manage lending, but to show why this was difficult in the 2000s. A structural bank liquidity glut made it difficult for the central bank to control interbank rates, and meant that many banks could expand their balance sheets without paying much attention to interbank market conditions.

[1] To the extent that bank cost functions vary with quantities, these problems infect the model's conclusions about relative interest rates, also. If costs are constant, quantities of credit and deposits are irrelevant to these conclusions so the problems have no impact on the determination of relative rates.

5.1 Beyond the Industrial Organisation Approach

The industrial organisation model is one of *stock* equilibrium on the bank side: equilibrium means that banks have optimised their balance sheets subject to the various constraints. But policymakers are interested in the *rate of growth* of credit and deposits. Since the model focuses on stock equilibrium, it gives comparative statics answers to such questions about changes in stocks. But on the non-bank side of the loan and deposit markets, Freixas and Rochet (2008, p. 75) refer to *flow* instead of stock concepts, representing the demand for funds in the loans market with an 'investment demand function', and the supply of funds in the deposit market with a 'savings function'. If this were all, the problem might be fixed simply by relabelling the functions to refer to stocks: the stock demand for bank loans, and the demand for deposits, abandoning the misleading identification of these with investment and saving flows. But the more fundamental problem is that these functions are not independent of one another.

Freixas and Rochet's (2008) model recognises the interdependence of bank behaviour in loan and deposit markets but fails to recognise that shifts in the loan market will affect the *demand* for deposits as well as supply. There are good reasons to believe that *both* the demand for and supply of deposits will be affected by bank lending, while reverse influences are much weaker. Therefore, we argue that rather than treat loan and deposit market conditions as mutually determining one another, it is better to see causality as running from loans to deposits—as argued by Sun (2015 [2001]), and as is implicit in the strategy of Chinese monetary policy.

Consider the supply of deposits first. We noted in Chapter 3 the claim of Yan and Li (2016, p. 192) that 'money is endogenous in the economy and uncontrollable by the central bank'. But the money stock is endogenous in the sense that it is affected by the demand for bank *credit*, not the demand for money itself.

An individual bank issues some quantity of deposits only in return for some specific asset from the depositor,[2] with the following effects on its individual balance sheet, and (in italics) the aggregate balance sheet of the banking system:

[2]We are informed here by the 'counterparts approach' to understanding change in the money supply (Goodhart 1989, pp. 151–155).

- Receipt from depositor at another bank (e.g., a cheque or electronic fund transfer order): A payment between customers of different banks involves the cancellation of deposits at the payer's bank and the creation of deposits at the payee's bank, and a transfer of reserves from one bank to another, but *no aggregate change in deposits or reserves.*
- Receipt from central bank: Payments from the central bank or from a government deposit at the central bank to a non-bank depositor *increase aggregate deposits and reserves.*
- Cash: A deposit of cash increases the bank's and *aggregate bank deposits and reserves, without directly affecting the broad money stock.*
- Foreign exchange: When a depositor converts foreign exchange into a domestic bank deposit, the bank can then exchange the foreign currency for reserves from the central bank at the pegged exchange rate. *Aggregate domestic deposits and reserves increase.*
- Securities: When a bank buys securities from a non-bank, *aggregate deposits increase, but not reserves.*
- Debt: The bank increases deposits in the borrower's account in exchange for the promise of repayment. *Aggregate deposits increase, but not reserves.* (In the case of an overdraft, aggregate deposits increase only once the borrower spends.)

Reverse transactions (payments to central bank or government, cash withdrawal, loan repayment, bond sales, etc.) have the opposite effects on aggregate deposits and reserves.

Most of the transactions with an influence on aggregate deposits are not at the discretion of enterprises and households. Net receipts from the government depend on fiscal policy.[3] Net foreign exchange conversion depends on the balance of payments, given the managed exchange rate. This leaves non-bank holdings of cash and securities. Any individual unit

[3]Note that fiscal deficits add to the money supply in the first instance even if matched by bond issuance, to the extent that the bonds are purchased by banks. When a non-bank purchases a bond from the Treasury or central bank, a deposit is cancelled and the unit's bank also loses reserves. But when a bank purchases a bond from the Treasury or central bank, bank reserves fall but no deposit is cancelled. However, the fall in bank reserves may have an indirect impact on deposits through its effect on bank liquidity, and therefore lending—but this depends on the state of the money market and monetary policy.

can convert between securities and deposits by selling or buying them to other units. But if both units are non-banks, deposits simply change hands: only transactions between non-banks and banks (including the central bank) affect *aggregate* deposits. As the PBC's Sun (2015 [2001], pp. 34–35) puts it,

> If a resident uses savings deposits for consumption, he or she has converted his savings deposits into consumer goods. But for the others, such behaviour increases savings deposits or cash or corporate deposits. In general, the money will not disappear… Similarly, residents making other forms of investments such as buying shares will not reduce the total amount of money. The amount of money will not decrease unless banks recover the loans.

There were few transactions of securities between banks and non-banks because of the mismatch between the kinds of securities held by banks and non-banks, respectively. Firms held few securities of any kind; household bond holdings were minuscule compared to typical annual deposit growth (see Tables 2.1 and 2.2). Equities became more important to households, at least by 2006/2007, but banks did not hold equities. This meant there was little scope for securities transactions between non-banks and banks to have an appreciable impact on the stock of deposits. The exception was banks' own issuance of bonds and shares, which had a noticeable but modest impact relative to other factors from mid-2004. (This can be seen in Fig. 5.1, where bank bond and equity issuance to non-banks are the main components of 'other items net (identified)'.)

Cash deposits and withdrawals could also have only a minimal effect on deposits: even if households converted their entire cash holdings into deposits at once, it would increase deposits by only around five to ten per cent, in a context where M2 was growing 15–20% per year.

Ultimately, then, the stock of deposits—and so of money as a whole—was driven mainly by three factors: bank lending, central bank accumulation of foreign exchange, and banking system accumulation of government debt. Figure 5.1 shows the relative importance of these factors to growth in the money stock. It is based on data from the PBC's 'depository corporation survey', which follows the principles of the International Monetary Fund's (2000) *Monetary and Financial Statistics*

Manual. This records the consolidated balance sheet of all financial institutions whose liabilities are included in the broad money supply (M2, i.e., demand and time/savings deposits plus currency held by non-bank, non-government units). This therefore includes the central bank along with other banks. Claims between these institutions—such as commercial bank reserves—are netted out so they do not appear on the aggregate balance sheet. The same applies to interbank claims. This allows us to focus on those balance sheet changes that are the counterparts to change in M2.

Figure 5.1 presents growth in M2 (the line) alongside quarterly change in each other balance sheet category (the bars). Balance sheet changes associated with the creation of money increase the height of the category's bar (increases in assets, decreases in non-monetary liabilities), and changes associated with the cancellation of money decrease it (decreases in assets, increases in non-monetary liabilities). Points on the M2 growth line therefore match the sum of the bars in each quarter, allowing us to decompose its growth into its counterpart balance sheet categories.

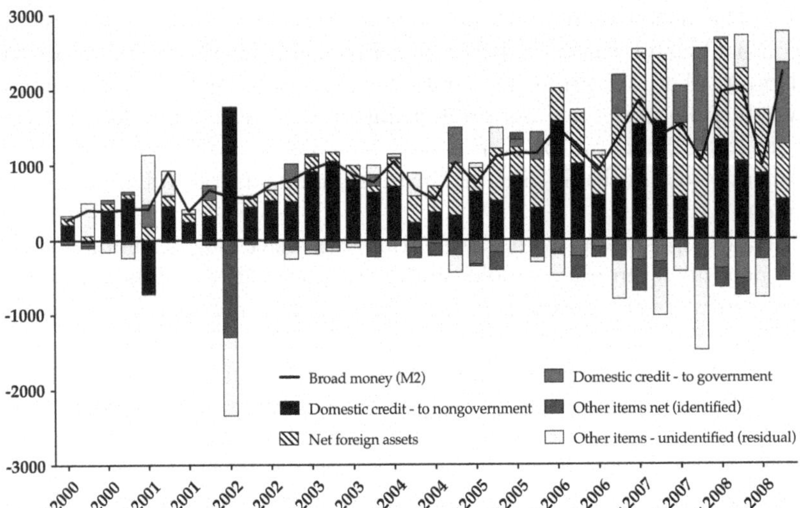

Fig. 5.1 Change in broad money and its bank sector balance sheet counterparts, RMB bn (quarterly) (*Source* PBC/CEIC, authors' calculations)

The data is far from perfect (see Appendix), but the outline is clear. In most quarters, most money growth can be explained by the expansion of bank claims on non-banks and the accumulation of foreign currency due to balance-of-payments surpluses.[4] Government debt was important in only a few quarters, and rarely a dominant factor. From 2006 on, the growth of non-deposit liabilities opened a substantial gap between broad money formation and banking system asset growth: that is, M2 grew more slowly than banking sector assets.

To summarise, the money stock was not responsive to demand, because there were few channels through which non-banks exchanged assets with banks *except* through the extension and repayment of credit. Purchases of foreign exchange were an important exception, but this had to do with the balance of payments rather than non-banks' demand for money.

Turning to the demand for deposits: Nobody is forced to hold them, of course, so one way or another voluntary demand must have been reconciled with this money stock. In China, as we have noted, the actual deposit interest rate tended to press against the regulatory ceiling. Without the ceiling, would bank expansion have been checked by a rising cost of funds as higher rates were necessary to induce non-banks to hold the resulting deposits? Not necessarily.

Freixas and Rochet's (2008) industrial organisation model treats the demand for deposits as a positive function of the deposit rate alone, implying that any increase in deposits—and therefore any expansion of aggregate bank balance sheets—must involve an increase in the deposit rate. This neglects the relationship between income and the demand for money: we would expect rising income to increase the demand for deposits, other things being equal.[5] If bank credit expansion facilitates an increase in investment and therefore income, it will also increase the demand for money: perhaps not to the full extent of the deposits created, but to

[4] Note that not all the bank credit category is loans: It also includes bank lending to non-bank financial institutions, on the interbank market and otherwise. This is separated in the data from 2002 and makes up around a tenth of the banking system's total domestic credit throughout our period. We have chosen not to treat it as a separate category for simplicity, as it grew roughly in line with all domestic credit.

[5] The demand for deposits is a component of the broader demand for money, which includes the demand for cash. As we have seen, the cash-deposit ratio declined steadily in China in the 2000s, suggesting that the liquidity or convenience premium of cash over deposits declined.

some extent. Further, besides income, the demand for money is normally treated as a function of *its yield relative to expected yields on alternative assets*, not of the absolute yield on money itself.[6] Putting income aside for the moment, this means a shift in the expected yield on other assets could play a role in reconciling an increased stock of deposits with demand. If non-banks respond to an increase in deposit holdings by adjusting their portfolios towards securities, these can increase in value until expected yields are low enough to induce people to hold the deposits. Indeed, since non-banks *in the aggregate* can reduce deposit holdings only through transactions with banks or the central bank, and such transactions were limited, it seems adjustment of securities prices rather than deposit rates must do most of the adjusting. With bonds held mainly by banks, the sharemarket (and real estate) was the outlet for such shifts. Since firms did not buy equities, and tended to passively hold deposits, we can see the effects in sectoral flow-of-funds accounts: Table 2.2 and 2.3 show that the household shift from deposits during the sharemarket boom of 2007 was matched by a roughly equivalent accumulation of deposits by firms.

Finally, we must consider how well a portfolio choice model of demand for money represents Chinese reality. Such a model presumes that non-banks regularly adjust their asset portfolios to maximise expected returns, including the implicit liquidity return from holding money as well as explicit monetary returns. But are deposits always deliberately held? Goodhart (1989, pp. 75–81) argues that a substantial part of money balances at a given point in time may represent 'buffer-stock' demand for money—not held *deliberately* but simply received and not yet spent. There are good reasons to believe this is an especially important category for understanding money holdings in 2000s China, that is, that non-banks were particularly passive in their deposit holding. As discussed in Chapter 3, estimates of demand-for-money functions in China have tended to find long run but not short-run relationships: a 'monetary overhang' of deposit holdings above that estimated by the model that may persist for many months (Gerlach and Kong 2005).[7] This is

[6]In Freixas and Rochet's model, the only alternative assets available to non-banks are Treasury bills, which they assume 'for simplicity' to be perfect substitutes for deposits, with the same interest rate in equilibrium (Freixas and Rochet 2008, p. 75). This assumes away the portfolio choice at the heart of standard conceptions of the demand for money.

[7]To recall, Gerlach and Kong (2005) found that the peak of transmission from a 'monetary shock' to prices came after 20 quarters, i.e., five years.

consistent with the idea that many non-bank units let deposits accumulate passively for some time, rather than always actively managing their asset portfolios. In Chinese conditions, such passivity is not necessarily irrational, given the paucity of alternative assets, especially capital-safe assets. Delatte (2008, p. 17) remarks that the money supply has grown faster than GDP since the 1980s because of a 'huge desire by Chinese to save by holding yuan and yuan denominated assets'—and an adequate supply of yuan-denominated assets other than deposits has not been forthcoming.

We also reiterate that firm deposit holdings are almost as large as those of households, though standard models typically ignore firm liquidity preference (Michell 2012, p. 244). Firms in the aggregate evidently borrowed substantially more than they needed to fund investment, and accumulated in deposits a large proportion of what they borrowed from banks. Since the interest rate on loans was around three percentage points higher than that on deposits, this seems puzzling—a high price to pay for liquidity. Of course, this is firms *in the aggregate*: the firms doing the borrowing need not be the firms accumulating the deposits. Michell (2012, pp. 244–247) explores the issue. On the one hand, individual firms may have had reasons to deliberately 'overcapitalise' (Toporowski 2008), issuing more liabilities than they need for investment purposes, and hoarding liquid assets—in part as a hedge to bridge potential gaps between uncertain revenue and contractual obligations. Even firms with current access to bank credit had reason to hoard for a rainy day, when policy might tighten. Alternatively, since the investment spending of one firm is the revenue of others, firms may more-or-less passively accumulate deposits—an enterprise form of Goodhart's 'buffer-stock' holdings. Aggregate deposit holdings would be a combination of the deliberate and the passive, and the line between the two is blurry anyway. The important point is that the deposits created when firms borrow remain deposits in someone's account, except to the extent that the associated flows induce deposit-cancelling transactions such as loan repayments. Michell treats the Chinese situation as a special case of Kalecki's (1965) picture of the dynamic relationship between borrowing, investment, profit and firms' deposits. In this case, firms' ultimate conversion from bank to long-term direct financing was blocked, because of the limited market for private securities: both firms and households tended to hold wealth in deposits, so finance remained bank-intermediated.

In summary, the industrial organisation treatment of banks as strategic rather than passive actors is a step forward from the money multiplier, but the approach also takes a step backwards in treating banks simply as intermediaries for 'funds' from savers to borrowers. Banking system expansion increases demand and supply for deposits simultaneously. In China, the extent of passive deposit holding and dearth of alternative assets left bank expansion especially unconstrained, except to the extent that it was checked by direct controls.

In other words, the industrial organisation approach rightly treats banks as active balance sheet managers, but misses the impact of the expansion of credit on the demand for, as well as supply of, deposits. If we merely 'completed' the industrial organisation model by extending its concern for balance sheet consistency to non-banks as well as banks, we would be left with an overdetermined model. Deposits created by credit expansion must be held by somebody. Not only must banks be satisfied with the composition of balance sheets, but so must firms and households—and how can we be sure both would be satisfied at the same combination of interest rates? As Goodhart (1989, pp. 228–229) puts it,

> one of the two aggregates, either bank deposits or bank loans, must vary to some extent passively as a residual in order to maintain the banks' balance sheet always in balance… [T]he demand for credit at given interest rates determines the stock of money—in theory the reverse might have been true, with the demand for money at given interest rates determining the volume of bank credit. In markets as they actually exist, it is the former, not the latter, that happens to be more generally true… [I]f one is concerned with a broad monetary aggregate, comprising the bulk of bank deposits, it is the demand for credit that, to use Keynes's phrase, 'rules the roost'. When the demand for credit rises at a given level of interest rates, the overall volume of broad money will rise in line.

In other words, the stock of bank deposits is endogenous in the sense that it responds to the demand for *credit*, but not to the demand for deposits or money more broadly.[8] The stock of money, determined mainly in the market for loans, must be voluntarily held. But as discussed above, much demand for deposits seems to be passive in the short run, so that no increase in deposit rates (relative to yields on other assets) is

[8] Chick and Dow (2002) present a series of models recognising this point and showing how the market for credit and for deposits interact.

necessary to induce agents to hold an increased stock. Even over a longer period, credit expansions will be expected to increase nominal income and so the demand for money.

We cannot presume, then, that rising deposit interest rates would have checked bank balance sheet expansion by raising the cost of funds. This is especially true in China, given the deposit rate ceiling, but would have been the case even without the ceiling. Given the state of liquidity preference of non-banks, the demand for deposits could be brought in line with bank expansion due to (1) passive 'buffer stock' holdings, at least in the short run; (2) rising demand due to rising income over the longer run; and (3) increasing asset prices to the extent that passive and income-related demand did not absorb the increase in supply.

The PBC's *Monetary Policy Report* for the fourth quarter of 2005 contained a primer on the relationship between loans and deposits. It shows thinking at the central bank was in line with the analysis we have presented here. It sought to counter an argument being made by some commentators that a gap between loans and deposits on bank balance sheets meant that banks had substantial unused lending capacity. This argument reflected a misunderstanding that banks' lending capacity depended on the deposits they attracted, so that an excess of deposits over loans meant spare lending potential. The report explained that it was the other way around; that loans created deposits:

> If we observe and analyse this phenomenon from the perspective of a single bank or part of the banking system, we inevitably will derive some implausible conclusions. In a banking system based on credit money, all money, including deposits and cash, is created by the central bank and commercial banks through loans and bond purchases, and then held by economic entities, such as enterprises and individuals. From the point of view of the banking system, assets, such as loans, are created before liabilities, such as deposits. In terms of the changes in the balance sheet, when issuing a loan, both the loans on the asset side and the deposits on the liability side increase by the same amount at the same time… The process of lending is also a process of deposit creation. (PBC 2005, p. 4)

In fact the widening gap between deposits and loans involved an increase in non-loan assets (bonds), loan write-offs, central bank accumulation of foreign exchange, and a slowdown in the growth of non-banks' demand for cash (PBC 2005, p. 5). The gap had nothing to do with unused lending capacity, because banks are not constrained by deposit-raising. Banks are constrained rather by ***liquidity***, 'and there is no direct linkage between such an excess [of deposits over loans] and banking liquidity' (p. 6). We now consider the nature of this liquidity constraint.

5.2 Bank Liquidity and Lending

In the absence of regulatory controls (including capital requirements), the ultimate constraint on the supply of bank credit is not banks' need to raise deposits, but their need to settle among themselves with reserves. It is 'in the requirement to settle net payments every day on the books of the central bank, we find the ultimate discipline for the entire system' (Mehrling 2011, p. 13). This is the essence of the 'money view', as described by Mehrling. This is a tradition of monetary thought from the perspective of central banks and watchers of central banks, and it seems to fit the views expressed by PBC policymakers, that 'the only constraint on lending activities is the requirement to hold reserves' (Sun 2015 [2001], p. 18).

With access to an interbank market, individual banks are not constrained by the quantity of their own reserves, because they can acquire them when needed by selling other assets or borrowing. The reserve constraint appears through the cost and availability of reserves on the interbank market, and this is a question of the state of supply and demand for reserves across the banking system as a whole, including the central bank's own activity. The ideal for Chinese central bankers in the 2000s was policy that would operate in the interbank market to manage liquidity conditions, controlling bank lending and the money supply indirectly: market-based policy, as in the West, but adapted for the particular institutional conditions of the Chinese financial system. In the next two chapters, we explain the problems on this front that led them back to heavier reliance on direct banking controls. But first here we explain the principles behind the ideal.

As discussed in the last section, banks create deposits, which are claims on themselves. But these claims are promises to pay reserves, which the bank must be ready to redeem when a depositor pays the depositor of another bank (or the central bank), withdraws cash, or purchases foreign exchange. In China, as in many other countries, banks are subject to a reserve requirement stipulating that they hold reserves amounting to a set proportion to deposits: six per cent at the beginning of the decade, increased later. The requirement did not need to be met continuously, but on particular dates three times per month (Geiger 2010, p. 82). A bank could fall below the requirement between reporting days, but if it came short on a reporting date, it faced a severe penalty—a fine amounting to six per cent of the shortfall per day until made good. The bank knew the quantity of required reserves in advance, because it was set relative to deposits ten days before the reporting date, but faced uncertainty about reserve flows over any given period. The bank would have a good idea of the probability distribution of inflows and outflows, given the quantity and average term of its deposits, but needed to either maintain a buffer of excess reserves or stand ready to draw from the interbank market as necessary to cover shortfalls. With deposit rates generally at the regulatory ceiling, banks could not attract deposits by raising rates.[9]

When a bank lends, it simultaneously issues a deposit claim upon itself to the borrower—there is no need to pre-fund the loan. But of course borrowers usually borrow to spend (though not necessarily immediately) and many of their payments will be made to customers of other banks, obliging the lending bank to transfer reserves. The lending bank is likely to lose reserves equal to some large proportion of the deposits it created with the loan. However, at the same time, other banks will also be lending, and the first bank will be receiving reserves through clearing as its depositors receive payments from customers of other banks. If the pattern of deposits among banks remains stable, a bank expanding lending at a faster rate than other banks would expect to see its reserves diminish, while a bank expanding more slowly would see reserves pile up. This is the source of the impression that banks need to raise deposits in order to lend: the lending of other banks tends to increase a bank's reserves, and so its lending capacity.

But the individual bank is not constrained by its current reserves, because it can obtain them at will by selling assets or borrowing (selling claims on itself) on the interbank market. Each bank may be indifferent about whether reserves accrue from depositors' incoming payments, from cash deposits, or from its own transaction with another bank. But

[9]There were other ways of competing for deposits: for example, He et al. (2015, p. 259) mention the development of 'tie-up' contracts, with which a lending bank could require borrowers to hold deposits with itself. Acharya et al. (2017, p. 17) mention gifts.

payments between bank depositors net out at the macro level, because one bank's reserve gain is another's loss. Deposits of cash from the non-bank public increase reserves for the whole banking system, but we have seen that this makes a minor difference at most and is not a factor banks have influence over (at least while unable to increase deposit interest rates). Thus the 'undifferentiated need for money' (Goodhart 1989, p. 227) for the individual bank aggregates into demand for *reserves* for banks as a whole. The interbank market is the focal point where total demand for reserves meets supply.

A paper by Sun (2015 [2004]) gives an understanding of how PBC economists at the time understood bank liquidity management. He writes that Chinese literature on liquidity management is 'almost non-existent' (p. 42), so his references are mainly to American work on the workings of the federal funds market in the United States (e.g., Poole [1970]; Feinman [1993], Strongin [1995], Hamilton [1997, 1998], Bernanke and Mihov [1998], and Meulendyke [1998]). The central bank can implement monetary policy through the interbank market by controlling the supply (or conditions of supply) of reserves, relative to demand. '[T]he monetary policy transmission process can to some extent be concentrated into a model of the reserves supply and demand relationship, which makes the analysis of monetary policy operations more simple and efficient' (Sun 2015 [2004], p. 44).

Sun distinguishes between a bank's *ex ante* and *ex post* demand for reserves. A bank makes medium-term plans for a particular level of excess reserves (i.e., above the volume of required reserves) in the context of its overall balance sheet management, including decisions about lending to non-banks, bondholding, and medium-term interbank market borrowing and lending. It makes this plan knowing that excess reserves at a given point in time will be uncertain, because of the uncertainty of reserve flows. Holding excess reserves means foregoing the additional interest available on other assets, but lessens the risk of needing to borrow to cover a reserve shortfall, at an unknown interest rate. Note that lending is a part of the medium-term decision, so that (expected) conditions in the interbank market influence the bank's lending.

There is no reason to expect that the aggregate of banks' *ex ante* (planned) demand for reserves matches the actual volume of reserves, but *ex post* holdings must equal *ex post* supply. Sun (2015 [2004], p. 46) reproduces a diagram from Meulendyke's (1998) analysis of the US federal funds market indicating the determinants of demand

and supply for reserves. Total reserve demand is composed of required and excess reserves. Required reserves are a simple function of the volume of deposits and the required reserve ratio. The demand for excess reserves depends on banks' assessment of their needs to fulfil withdrawals and clearing of depositors' payments to the customers of other banks—which is subject to uncertainty and with the risk of costs from falling short weighed against the higher return on other assets. Total reserve supply is made up of reserves borrowed from the central bank, and reserves not borrowed from the central bank—but Sun suggests a distinction between 'spontaneous' and 'policy' supply would be more useful in a Chinese context. The former are reserves issued in transactions not under the control of monetary policymakers, such as the central bank's purchases of foreign exchange, required by exchange rate management. The latter are transactions undertaken for policy reasons, whether targeting a stock or an interest rate.

Interbank interest rates adjust until demand matches supply. Adjustment may take place on the supply side as well as the demand side: the central bank may or may not deliberately accommodate demand at a given interest rate with open market operations, supported by standing facilities (such as the PBC's rediscount facility) lending reserves on demand (in return for good collateral) at a predetermined rate. Thus there is *ex ante* and *ex post* supply as well as demand for reserves, with *ex ante* supply arising from 'spontaneous' factors like foreign exchange purchases and monetised public deficits, and *ex post* supply incorporating central bank reactions to interbank market conditions. *Ex post* conditions in the money market—the quantity of reserves held by each bank, and the pattern of interest rates—then feed back into banks' medium-term planning. Banks cannot adjust their lending quickly, so that other parts of the balance sheet must adjust in the short run, but over time banks will respond to interbank market tightness and/or volatility by slowing their lending, provided they expect these conditions to last.

So far, this seems a promising domain for the exercise of policy. By adjusting the policy supply of reserves *ex post* in response to bank demand for reserves, the central bank can establish the interest rate it wants in the interbank market, and so hopefully influence the supply of credit and thereby deposits. However, the Chinese banking system had a structural liquidity surplus in the 2000s: a large quantity of excess reserves which the central bank had difficulty absorbing. Individual Chinese banks tended to hold large buffers of excess reserves, which left them able to sustain substantial reserve outflows without being forced to restrain their lending, and were not very responsive to changing interbank interest rates in the short run. As discussed in Chapter 4, and shown in Fig. 4.2, the banking system as a whole held large stocks of excess reserves.

This is an anomaly for both the money multiplier and the industrial organisation approaches. The money multiplier model presumes that banks are 'fully loaned up', in the sense that they do not hold reserves beyond those set by the required reserve-deposit ratio. (Or if they do hold excess reserves, these are themselves at a constant ratio to deposits.) Freixas and Rochet (2008, pp. 70–71) also see no reason for banks to hold excess reserves. Porter and Xu (2016, pp. 152–153), however, bring excess reserves into their bank profit maximisation equation. In their model, each bank has a target level of excess reserves. They trade off the implicit cost of falling short of their target against the opportunity cost of holding alternative assets with a higher return. This is essentially a bank liquidity preference function: a schedule relating demand for excess reserves to the interbank interest rate, given the rate of return on excess reserves, expectations about reserve flows, the level of uncertainty about those flows, willingness to bear liquidity risk, etc.

This is a more sophisticated take on the demand for reserves, which can deal with variations in excess reserve holdings without undermining the framework of balance sheet optimisation. But it suggests more determinacy in bank reserve demand than PBC authorities believed there was in reality—and without that determinacy, policy becomes more difficult than the framework implies. Sun (2015 [2004]) noted that many Chinese banks did not seem to act like the maximisers of theory, continually adjusting their reserve holdings in response to changes in interest rates. Just as their depositors tended to passively allow a buffer of deposit holdings to fluctuate, at least in the short run, so did the banks themselves with reserves. When a bank experiences a net inflow or outflow of reserves, it does not know at first whether it reflects a random fluctuation or a more fundamental shift in circumstances. At first, it allows its buffer of excess reserves to absorb changes, 'mainly because the cost brought about by a short-term increase or decrease in reserves is lower than the adjustment cost of commercial banks' (Sun 2015 [2004], p. 45). The expected gains of more active engagement in the money market were apparently not enough to overcome the cost of that engagement, especially where it was quite possible that one week's net flows will be reversed the next. The optimising bank of the model has no reason not to lend spare reserves on the interbank market even for a day at a time, so long as rates exceeded the return on excess reserves by enough to cover transaction costs and compensate for any risk. Some Chinese banks may have been managing their liquidity like this—there was, after all, an active market in one-day repos—but evidently banks in general were satisficers rather than maximisers. They were willing to let excess reserves fluctuate within a wide range.

Only when a bank believes that a shift in reserves represents a lasting change, rather than a short-term or random and reversible fluctuation, will it react by adjusting their overall balance sheet. The parameters in the bank's *ex ante* reserve demand function shift accordingly—and this may affect the bank's willingness to lend. (Or it may not, if the bank adapts mainly by adjusting its portfolio of non-loan investments, intermediate in liquidity between reserves and loans.) The existence of the buffers gave banks considerable time to adjust to shifts that did turn out to reflect longer term trends. They 'are inclined to adopt a "tolerance" method in reaction, in which they change the parameters of the reserves demand function to digest the unintentional reserves change…[so that] it is difficult for the central bank's policy to be transmitted within the banking system' (Sun 2015 [2004], p. 63).

Sun argues that there is an asymmetry in central bank control of interbank market conditions: Authorities have more power when they control the flow of reserves to banks than when they have to mop up excess reserves the banks already have. Money-market-oriented policy can be more precise and powerful where the banking system depends on borrowing from the central bank to meet its reserve needs. As a lender, the bank can dictate terms. If the banking system faces a structural liquidity deficit (*ex ante* reserve demand exceeds supply), banks on the whole cannot expand by running down buffers, and the central bank can control the marginal cost of reserves (Sun 2015 [2004], 46). When the banks enjoy a structural surplus of reserves, on the other hand, the central bank comes to market as just another trader, rather than a monopoly supplier, and 'has no decisive effect on interest rates' (Sun 2015 [2004], 63). Its operations may simply be absorbed by the buffers, and it may need to engage at a large scale to move the market in the desired direction, with uncertainty around magnitude and lags.

There were thus two slippages between policy action in the interbank market and the ultimate targets, loans and deposits. First, as just discussed, the central bank had difficulty controlling interbank market rates in conditions of structural liquidity surplus. Second, the existence of large reserve buffers meant that many banks had considerable room to expand lending without needing to worry about interbank market conditions anyway. Contrary to the Freixas-Rochet model, the interbank rate did not represent the marginal cost of lending (Green 2005, pp. 10–14).

Effective market-based policy depended on moving the banking system from a position of structural liquidity surplus to structural deficit—but this was easier said than done. In Sun's terms, the 'spontaneous' supply of reserves was difficult for policy action to reabsorb. In the next chapter we explain why, and follow the PBC's reaction.

Appendix: Note on Figure 5.1

Figure 5.1 is based on the PBC's 'depository corporation survey', which follows the principles of the International Monetary Fund's (2000) *Monetary and Financial Statistics Manual*. This records the consolidated balance sheet of all financial institutions whose liabilities are included in the broad money supply (M2, i.e., demand and time/savings deposits plus currency held by non-bank, non-government units). This sectoral balance sheet can be used to decompose the balance sheet counterparts to growth in broad money. The basic equation in the *Manual*'s framework for decomposing change in the money stock is:

$$\Delta BML = \Delta NFA + \Delta NCG + \Delta CORS - \Delta OIN$$

where *BML* is broad money liabilities, *NFA* net foreign assets, *NCG* net banking sector claims on government, *CORS* claims on other resident sectors (primarily firms and households), and *OIN* other items net. This last category is a residual representing the banking sector's non-monetary liabilities (e.g., bonds and owners' equity) less other assets. As a residual category, it also includes any discrepancy between recorded liabilities and recorded assets.

In other words, in any given period the change in broad money will be equal to the sum of the change in the sector's net foreign assets, the change in claims on government, and the change in claims on non-bank, non-government units, less the change in the sector's net other items.

In our figure, the line traces the growth in broad money growth. The bars represent changes in its balance sheet counterparts. In each period, then, the point on the line will fall at the sum of the counterpart bars. Growth in net asset categories (*NFA*, *NGC*, and *CORS*) is represented by a positive bar, while a fall in these categories is represented by a negative bar. Conversely, because it is on the same side of the balance sheet as money, growth in net other liability categories (*OIN*) is represented by a negative bar, while a fall in these categories is represented by a positive bar.

There is unfortunately a substantial unidentified gap between assets and liabilities in the depository corporation survey data, which raises problems for interpretation. We have highlighted this by separating the *OIN* into two categories, one representing identifiable non-monetary liabilities, and the other an unidentified residual category. The identified non-monetary liabilities include (i) deposits excluded from broad money (perhaps including the deposits of some non-bank financial institutions and local governments), (ii) bank bonds, and (iii) paid-in capital. The residual category corresponds to the 'liability: other' category in the PBC's depository corporation survey. It must include miscellaneous liabilities such as retained earnings (owners' equity excluding paid-in capital). But note that this category was *negative* until the third quarter of 2007, so that unidentified assets must exceed unidentified liabilities.

This makes interpreting change in this category difficult, especially in the absence of any official comment. The figure will reflect not only actual movements in unidentified balance sheet categories, but also changes in identification. There is good reason to believe that the periods of major change in this category usually reflect data categorisation issues rather than something more substantial—it always has a counterpart in an unusual change in another category.

In the first quarter of 2001, the jump in the residual category corresponds with a large fall in recorded claims on non-government units—the only fall for this category in the whole series. This apparent decline in bank claims on firms and households does not appear in the PBC's separate data series on loans (CEIC series code 7029101, CKAHLA) or the flow-of-funds accounts (CEIC series code 1819401, CAACBU). This suggests it is an artefact of classification.

The large fall in the residual in the first quarter of 2002 coincides with a known change in data classification. In this quarter, two new categories were added to the depository corporations survey balance sheet: 'claims on other [i.e., non-bank] financial institutions' on the asset side, and 'deposits excluded from broad money' on the liability side. The outcome was a simultaneous large fall in the residual 'other liabilities' category and increase in domestic credit (which we have combined into the 'domestic credit - to nongovernment' item) as a large volume of what had been unidentified was allocated to the new categories. This does not fully explain the changes in the residual category that quarter, but we can assume that other classification changes also took place. Discrepancies may also have arisen from lags associated with the sharp rise in central bank foreign exchange purchases.

Finally, the large fall in the residual category in the last quarter of 2007 coincides with an unusually large increase in bank claims on government. We presume, but cannot prove, that this involved a reclassification of some form of official debt.

Our main claim is not undermined by these difficulties. Over the whole period, most change in money growth corresponds to growth in net foreign assets and bank lending to firms and households, rather than increasing government debt. Movements in the unexplained residual were often small, particularly between mid-2002 and mid-2006, and we have suggested that the large jumps outside this timeframe were largely artefacts of data reclassification. It is worth noting, however, the modest but real role of growth in *identified* non-monetary liabilities—especially bank bond and equity issuance—in widening the gap between banking system assets and money supply from mid-decade. This is much more important than growth in 'deposits excluded from broad money'.

References

Acharya, Viral V., Jun Qian, and Zhishu Yang. 2017. "In the shadow of banks: Wealth management products and issuing banks' risk in China." Unpublished paper. Available at https://jrc.princeton.edu/sites/jrc/files/qian_jun-shadowbank-china-aqy-10feb17-all.pdf. 17 May 2019.

Bernanke, Ben S., and Ilian Mihov. 1998. "The liquidity effect and long-run neutrality." NBER Working Paper 6608.

Chick, Victoria, and Sheila Dow. 2002. "Monetary policy with endogenous money and liquidity preference: A nondualistic treatment." *Journal of Post Keynesian Economics* 24 (4), pp. 587–607.

Delatte, Anne-Laure. 2008. "Monetary policy and macrocontrol in China: The actual impact of window guidance." Unpublished paper. Available at http://citeseerx.ist.psu.edu/viewdoc/download?doi=10.1.1.651.7744&rep=rep1&type=pdf. 15 April 2019.

Feinman, Joshua. 1993. "Estimating the open market desk's daily reaction function." *Journal of Money, Credit and Banking* 25 (2), pp. 231–247.

Freixas, Xavier, and Jean-Charles Rochet. 2008. *Microeconomics of banking*. Cambridge, MA: MIT Press.

Geiger, Michael. 2010. *Monetary policy in China: Institutions, targets, instruments and strategies*. Dissertation, Bayerischen Julius-Maximillians-Universistat Wurzburg.

Gerlach, Stefan, and Janet Kong. 2005. "Money and inflation in China." Hong Kong Monetary Authority Research Memorandum 04/2005.

Goodhart, Charles A. E. 1989. *Money, information, and uncertainty*. Houndmills: Macmillan.

Green, Stephen. 2005. "Making monetary policy work in China: A report from the money market front line." Stanford Center for International Development Working Paper 245.

Hamilton, James D. 1997. "Measuring the liquidity effect." *American Economic Review* 87 (1), pp. 80–97.

Hamilton, James D. 1998. "The supply and demand for Federal Reserve deposits." *Carnegie-Rochester Conference Series on Public Policy* 49 (1), pp. 45–52.

He, Dong, Honglin Wang, and Xiangrong Yu. 2015. "Interest rate determination in China: Past, present, and future." *International Journal of Central Banking* 11 (4), pp. 255–277.

International Monetary Fund. 2000. *Monetary and financial statistics manual*. Washington, DC: International Monetary Fund.

Kalecki, Michal. 1965. *Theory of economic dynamics*. London: Unwin University Books.

Mehrling, Perry. 2011. *The New Lombard Street: How the Fed became the dealer of last resort*. Princeton: Princeton University Press.

Meulendyke, Ann-Marie. 1998. *US monetary policy and financial markets*. New York: Federal Reserve Bank of New York.

Michell, Jo. 2012. *Credit and investment in China: A flow-of-funds analysis*. PhD thesis, SOAS, University of London.

People's Bank of China. 2005. *Monetary Policy Report, Quarter 4*. Beijing: People's Bank of China.

Poole, William. 1970. "Optimal choice of monetary policy instruments in a simple stochastic monetary model." *Quarterly Journal of Economics* 84, pp. 197–216.

Porter, Nathan, and TengTeng Xu. 2016. "Money-market rates and retail interest regulation in China: The disconnect between interbank and retail credit conditions." *International Journal of Central Banking* 12 (1), pp. 143–198.

Strongin, Steven. 1995. "The identification of monetary policy disturbances explaining the liquidity puzzle." *Journal of Monetary Economics* 35, pp. 463–497.

Sun, Guofeng. 2015. *Reforms in China's monetary policy: A frontbencher's perspective*. New York: Palgrave Macmillan.

Toporowski, Jan. 2008. "Excess capital and liquidity management." Levy Economics Institute Working Paper 549.

Yan, Qingmin, and Jianhua Li. 2016. *Regulating China's shadow banks*. Milton Park: Routledge.

CHAPTER 6

Instruments I: Sterilisation and Interest Rate Controls

Abstract This is the first of a pair of chapters discussing how Chinese monetary policymakers deployed the instruments they had in the 2000s, and how their strategy evolved. It builds on earlier chapters, which established both how a potential transmission mechanism from interbank market through bank balance sheets might work, and why it was limited in practice. Here we discuss the difficulties posed by a large net foreign currency inflow, and the relationship between administered and market rates. The central bank's large-scale foreign exchange purchases left the banking system with a persistent structural liquidity surplus, which the central bank struggled to absorb. It first introduced central bank bills and then turned to intensive use of a variable reserve-deposit ratio to quarantine reserves. We discuss the extent to which policy-set and regulated bank rates influenced those rates left to be determined in the interbank market.

Keywords Monetary policy · China · Central banking · Sterilisation · Foreign exchange · Transmission

We are now in a position to discuss the details of how policy actually worked in the 2000s. We focus particularly on monetary restraint between 2002 and 2008, since this was what tested the new framework and drove its further transformation. The prioritisation of price stability affirmed in the mid-1990s was followed by a period of externally

M. Beggs and L. Deer, *Remaking Monetary Policy in China*,
https://doi.org/10.1007/978-981-13-9726-4_6

triggered deflation during and after the Asian financial crisis of 1997–1998 and the global downturn of 2001–2002, in which policy was set for monetary ease (Shu and Ng 2010, pp. 10–11). Only from the end of 2002 did policy begin to tighten. It is from this point that the PBC 'appears to have engaged in a regime that looks a lot like formal inflation targeting' (Girardin et al. 2017, pp. 2–3). There were two waves of inflation (see Table 7.1 in the next chapter): a moderate burst in 2003 (CPI inflation 3.2% over the year) and 2004 (2.4%); and a stronger burst in 2006–2007 (with CPI inflation 6.5% over 2007). The central bank continued to pursue restraint until the second half of 2008, when the global financial crisis provoked a sharp turn to stimulus.

We present this across two chapters. In Sect. 6.1, we discuss the difficulties posed for policy by the large net foreign currency inflow, and the central bank's response. Section 6.2 covers the relationship between administered and market interest rates. With the stage set, Chapter 7 then tracks the search for an effective policy strategy in the interbank market, and explains the return to heavier use of direct banking controls.

6.1 'Freezing Liquidity': Central Bank Bills and Reserve Requirements

The main obstacle to interbank-market-based monetary policy in China was the structural liquidity surplus of the banking system. In spite of this, the PBC found itself continuing to flood the banks with reserves because of the net purchases of foreign exchange mandated by exchange rate management. In Sun's (2015 [2004]) terms (see Sect. 5.2), the 'spontaneous' factors contributing to the supply of reserves were very challenging for 'policy' factors to overcome.

The government was committed to an exchange rate peg to the US dollar (from 2005, a crawling peg by which the renminbi was allowed to slowly appreciate against the US dollar). The peg obliged the central bank to exchange domestic currency for foreign currency at the set rate. As discussed in Sect. 5.1, central bank net purchases of foreign exchange increased both bank deposits and reserves. Dealing with the consequences of the large inflow of foreign exchange from 2003 forced policy to adapt. The size of the impact of foreign exchange purchases on bank reserves was such that there was no chance of fine management of bank liquidity before policymakers found effective means of sterilisation.

Michell (2012, pp. 168–169) argues that China fits neither 'asset-based' not 'overdraft' models of the relationship between the central bank and the banking system.[1] Rather, it has a 'foreign exchange based financial system'. As in an asset-based system, the banks are net creditors to the central bank, but most change in their reserves comes as a result of the central bank's passive foreign exchange purchases, rather than open market operations in government debt. The PBC did not *first* sterilise the consequences of international payments surpluses *then* engage in domestic policy. To some extent foreign exchange purchases created reserves that the PBC would have provided anyway to allow reserves to grow in line with the needs of a growing economy. Foreign exchange purchases were an exogenous variable, imposed by the exchange rate target and the balance of payments, to which policy adapted in pursuit of domestic targets.

Figure 6.1 illustrates the relationship between the central bank's net foreign exchange purchases, domestic transactions, and bank reserves. It is similar in construction to Fig. 5.1, except that it focuses on the change in bank reserves rather than money, and so presents changes on the central bank balance sheet rather than the balance sheet of the whole banking sector. To simplify, we display only bank reserves (including cash held by banks) rather than the whole monetary base (which includes cash in

[1]This distinction is made by Godley and Lavoie (2007, pp. 55–56, 374–375). In an asset-based financial system, there is a large stock of government debt outstanding, the banking system is a net creditor of the central bank, banks manage their liquidity by adjusting their asset holdings, and the central bank conducts open market operations in government debt. In an overdraft-based system, the banking system is a net borrower from the central bank, and banks generally manage their liquidity through borrowing, often through repurchase agreements with the central bank. Lavoie and Wang (2012, pp. 292–293) argue that China fits the overdraft category, because the central bank has a relatively small stock of government debt and substantially larger stock of claims on the banking system. We agree with Michell (2012, p. 169) that this is a mischaracterisation, because it neglects banks' claims on the central bank: Their reserves dwarf the PBC's claims on banks, so that the banking system is a net creditor to the central bank. Further, as Lavoie and Wang themselves note, some of the PBC's loans to the banking system are 'linked to the bailout of non-performing loans made by state-owned banks in the 1990s and are unlikely to be retrieved' (Lavoie and Wang 2012, p. 293)—and so quite different in form to the central bank liquidity provision in overdraft systems.

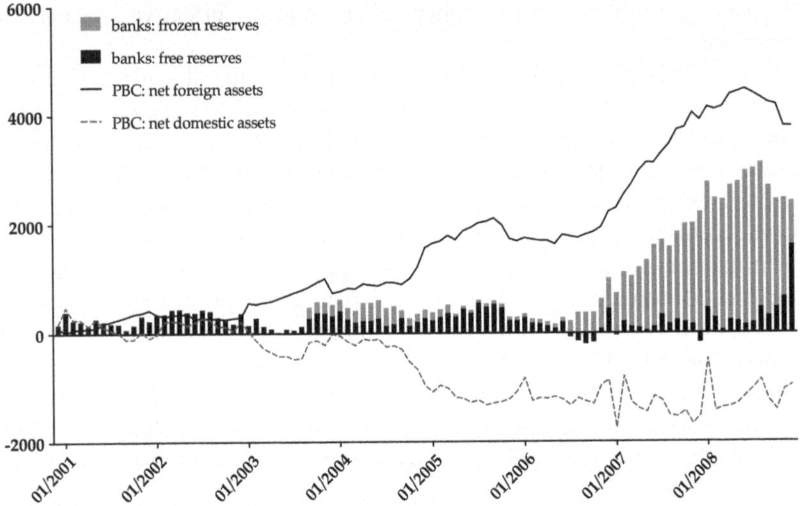

Fig. 6.1 Change in central bank net assets and bank reserves, year-on-year, RMB bn (*Source* PBC/CEIC, authors' calculations)

the hands of non-banks), and have consolidated PBC assets into 'net foreign' and 'net domestic' assets.

The higher line (higher, at least, from mid-2001) shows the year-on-year change in the central bank's net foreign assets, i.e., foreign assets less foreign liabilities. For the most part, this represents its accumulation of foreign currency from its maintenance of the exchange rate peg. The lower line shows the change in net domestic assets, excluding cash and bank reserves from the liability side.[2] The bars show the increase in bank reserves—including both bank cash and reserve deposits held with the central bank. They nearly equal the sum of the two lines—but not quite, as we have excluded the category of cash held by non-banks, which is a liability to the central bank but not part of bank reserves. With this exception, changes in bank reserves reflect the difference between changes in the central bank's net foreign assets and its net domestic assets, excluding its monetary liabilities.

[2]Net domestic assets include claims on government, depository corporations, other financial corporations, and non-financial institutions and other assets, less bills issued by the PBC itself and other domestic liabilities besides cash and reserve deposits.

The PBC had little control over its net foreign assets, but some control over its net domestic assets. It was not in complete control of the latter, because some other commitments interfered with what it might have chosen if focused solely on its macroeconomic targets. For example, it ran a rediscount facility through which banks could discount bills at a fixed rate. More importantly, it was still making substantial long-term loans unconnected to broader monetary policy, such as those involved in restructuring banks' bad debt, and others intended to subsidise rural credit cooperatives and the policy banks (Geiger 2010, pp. 92–93; Xie 2004, pp. 20–21). This lending could at times have an impact on the monetary base comparable to purchases of foreign exchange, at least before the latter's explosion after 2003. But the central bank could offset both foreign currency purchases and 'spontaneous' domestic lending by altering other balance sheet elements that were subject to monetary policy control—for example, by engaging in open market operations and issuing its own bills. Figure 6.1 shows that in general changes in net domestic assets offset changes in net foreign assets, but the sterilisation was not complete.

From 1998 to 2000, domestic open market operations fed reserves into the banking system, but over the next two years domestic operations often turned to withdrawing the reserves created by the PBC's foreign exchange purchases, as international payments surpluses mounted. From 2003, domestic operations were almost entirely dedicated to withdrawing reserves (Geiger 2008, p. 10; Sun 2015, p. 135). Until then, the PBC mainly worked with repo (repurchase agreements) and reverse repo transactions involving government and policy bank bonds.

While most central banks have traditionally operated with Treasury bonds 'because there is never any shortage of them' (Stigum and Crescenzi 2007, p. 347), the PBC began to find the supply of government bonds grossly inadequate for sterilisation purposes. Its open market operations mainly involved repurchase and reverse-repurchase agreements rather than outright exchanges, and it needed a stock of assets with which to work. Government debt typically made up the bulk of central bank assets in central banks elsewhere, but claims on government were only 5.5% of PBC assets as of the beginning of 2002 (CEIC/PBC Monetary Authority balance sheet; Bell and Feng 2013, p. 171). That year, the *increase* in the central bank's foreign exchange holdings was one-and-a-half times its *total* stock of government debt, and much bigger inflows were on the way. The PBC also used policy bank (see

Sect. 2.5) bonds in open market operations, but these too would soon be dwarfed by foreign exchange inflows.[3]

In response, the PBC began to issue its own bills, beginning with a conversion of outstanding repos to bills in September 2002 and holding open market auctions the following May (Green 2005, p. 4; Sun 2015, p. 135). These became the main instrument for open market operations (Gabor 2012, p. 359; Geiger 2008, pp. 9–11)—almost entirely responsible for the negative growth in net domestic assets after 2002 (as a liability, bills are a negative within the net domestic category). This amounted to large scale public borrowing not to fund expenditure but simply to absorb liquidity created by foreign exchange purchases.

But as its foreign assets continued to mount, the PBC had difficulty sterilising them even with its own bills. It could offer these at will, but not necessarily force feed them to the market. It had to let yields on the bills move dramatically in order to get institutions to buy them in enough quantity—after rising a full percentage point in 2004, they dropped more than two points over the following year before regaining 1.5 percentage points by mid-2006 (Ma et al. 2011, pp. 9–10). A PBC report that year complained that open market operations worked 'only at a "shallow" level' (PBC 2006a, p. 9), insufficient for sterilising the scale of foreign exchange purchases at the time. This is a cryptic remark, but Sun's (2015 [2004]) earlier paper helps us to understand the problem the PBC was referring to. Open market operations obviously depend on the willingness of counterparties to take the offered transactions. If banks were determined to keep open the lending capacity the increase in reserves made possible, central bank bill yields would have to rise towards lending rates to make them attractive:

[3] Policy bank bonds are not a separate category on the monetary authority's balance sheet, but we presume they make up a large part of the 'claims on other [i.e., non-depository] financial corporation' category. As of January 2002, the first month for which official data reports total assets, the PBC held RMB272.6bn of claims on government, and RMB706.5bn of claims on 'other financial corporations', out of total assets of RMB4531.1bn. (Compare to *growth* in foreign assets of RMB338.3bn in 2002, RMB741.7 in 2003, and RMB1573.9bn in 2004.) Most of its other assets were comprised of foreign exchange (RMB1900.6bn) and claims on depository institutions (RMB999.6bn). The latter included substantial loans to banks involved in restructuring bad debt, not easily recallable for monetary policy purposes.

> the central bank can only reduce the bond price continuously to increase the yield to a level similar to banks' lending yield after taking risk factors into account... This operation will lead to great fluctuations in the market interest rate level, which the central bank will find difficult to accept... Then the central bank's liquidity target may become difficult to realise or may be realised at high cost. (Sun 2015 [2004], pp. 52–53)

The central bank may find a willing partner at *some* interest rate, but it may not be willing to drive rates to that level. Higher domestic rates risked intensifying the foreign exchange inflows authorities were trying to sterilise (Lardy 2008, p. 4).[4] Further, falling bond prices erode confidence in bonds if banks expect them to fall further still, making them harder to market, even as interest costs to the central bank rise (Sun 2015 [2004], pp. 57–58).[5] Even after almost a decade of growth in the interbank market, Forssbaeck and Oxelheim (2007, p. 271) concluded that it remained too shallow for effective open market operations: 'the pricing mechanism does not work'.

Still, the interbank market was becoming much more active, thanks in part to the availability of the central bank bills themselves: a large pool of safe, short-term assets the market had previously lacked (see Table 2.5). The continued maturation of the money market was welcome to policymakers—the promise of open market operations depended on it—but they also worried that easily saleable official bills were nearly as liquid for banks as reserves themselves (PBC 2006a, p. 9; 2006b, p. 47; Li et al. 2007; Sun 2015 [2004], pp. 58–60).[6]

[4]Rising US interest rates from 2004 to 2006 relieved this tension to some degree (Yin 2007, p. 167), along with the downward movement of the exchange rate peg from mid-2005, and the PBC believed it could allow domestic rates to rise also with less impact on capital flows. But the concern remained.

[5]For example, Green (2005, p. 6) reports an episode in 2002 in which the PBC found itself having to purchase 7.8bn yuan worth of newly issued government bonds. Banks were only willing to purchase them at a substantially higher yield, leaving the underwriters open to large losses before the central bank stepped in. This relates to government bonds rather than central bank bills, but illustrates the general principle.

[6]Sterilisation by issuing bills was also costly in that the central bank normally pays a higher interest rate on bills than on reserves. This has sometimes made it prohibitively difficult for developing countries to sterilise large payments surpluses. In China's case, however, the central bank earned much more interest holding its reserves in US Treasury bonds than it paid on the bills (Prasad 2008, pp. 81–85; Geiger 2010, pp. 125–129). Nevertheless, sterilisation by raising the required reserve ratio would save the PBC

With pledged repo—the dominant form of repurchase agreements in China—the lender was not able to trade the collateral bond it temporarily held, so when the central bank entered into a reverse repo, the counterparty bank gave up liquidity for the full term. In contrast, selling bills to the banks left them with an instrument they could resell if short of reserves (Green 2005, p. 6).[7] If banks consider bills a close substitute for reserves, replacing one with the other may have little impact on their willingness to lend.

Policymakers' response was to turn to a direct control on bank balance sheets: the adjustable required reserve ratio (RRR). If open market operations were too 'shallow' to deal with the size of reserve fluctuations, 'the reserve requirement has the capacity to "deeply" freeze liquidity' (PBC 2006a, p. 9). Rather than absorbing the reserves created by the currency inflow, an increased reserve requirement kept them sitting inertly on bank balance sheets. This was entirely at the discretion of policymakers—unlike open market operations, with which the banks had to be willing participants. The impact of this instrument can be seen above in Fig. 6.1. The lighter portion of the bars represent the part of the change in monetary base absorbed by changes in required reserves. The darker portion of the bars thus represent the *adjusted* change in the monetary base, taking into account the effect of changes in the required reserve ratio; in other words, it shows changes in *free* reserves (including vault cash).[8] The PBC raised the ratio once in 2003 (from 6 to 7%) and once in 2004

considerable interest payments compared with bill issuance and made the exchange rate peg still more profitable (Ma et al. 2011, pp. 9–10).

[7] In China, collateralised repos do not involve the underlying asset legally changing hands. 'Outright' repos—much less common—do involve a change of hands and facilitate short-selling, for example (Green 2005, p. 9).

[8] In calculating the adjusted base we have followed the procedure used by Ma et al. (2011, pp. 7–8), based on Burger and Rasche (1977). We have adjusted the raw monetary base by adding or subtracting the bank reserves 'locked up' or released by RRR changes. Adjusted reserves (r(adj)) are defined as:

$$\mathrm{r(adj)} = D(t) \times (\mathrm{RRR}(0) - \mathrm{RRR}(t))$$

where $D(t)$ represents bank deposits in the current period, and RRR(0) and RRR(t) represent the required reserve ratio in the base period (December 1999) and the current period, respectively.

(to 7.5%).[9] From 2006, it began to make much more regular adjustments—on a more-or-less monthly basis—and engaged in open market operations multiple times per week.

In 2007, the central bank made heavy use of another 'deep freeze' tool: the issuance of 'special central bank bills' (Geiger 2010, p. 86). Though they took the form of PBC bills, they were not open market operations properly speaking, because target institutions were required to purchase them. Unlike shifts in the required reserve ratio, the special bills allowed the authorities to discriminate and lock up reserves at targeted individual banks considered to be expanding too fast. An official report claimed that 'the measure not only withdrew liquidity but served as a warning to banks with high credit growth' (PBC 2007a, p. 16). Later in the year, the central bank also increased the higher reserve ratio applying to banks that did not meet capital adequacy standards (PBC 2007b, p. 14).

The turn to heavier use of required reserve ratio adjustment and special bills transformed the central bank's tactics in the money market. The need to sterilise the effects of its foreign exchange purchases interfered with authorities' desire to guide interbank market interest rates. The 'spontaneous' contributions to reserve growth were so large that the effects of 'policy' contributions on interbank interest rates were too unpredictable. Once variations in the required ratio could be used to 'deeply freeze' reserves, open market operations could be turned to more delicate tasks, as we discuss in Sect. 7.1. First, though, we must consider another part of the context in which interbank market rates were determined: those rates directly controlled by policy.

6.2 'Dual-Track': Market and Administered Interest Rates

Chinese authorities did not have the tight control over interbank market interest rates enjoyed by many of their counterparts elsewhere, even after the turn to 'deep freezing' liquidity with reserve requirements. The precision of open market operations was challenged by the tendency

[9] In April 2004, the PBC also began to differentiate among banks with respect to required reserves: Banks that did not meet capital adequacy targets were subject to a ratio 0.5 percentage points higher than the standard, while urban and rural credit cooperatives enjoyed a ratio 1.5 percentage points lower (PBC 2004; Geiger 2010, pp. 81–82; Green 2005, p. 6). Our calculations for Fig. 6.1 use the standard ratio, as data is not available on the distribution of reserves and deposits among bank types.

of banks to passively allow their buffer stocks to absorb shifts in excess reserves, as discussed in Sect. 5.2. Lacking full control, the PBC coordinated its instruments to smooth volatility and *influence* interbank rates rather than control them precisely. The authorities did directly set some rates, however, which formed limits and benchmarks in the interbank market. Before discussing policy tactics with open market operations, we discuss the relationship between administered and market rates: China's 'dual-track' interest rate structure (He and Wang 2012).

To the extent that instruments with administered rates were substitutes for interbank market instruments, the rates must influence one another. Since administered rates were under the control of authorities, the direction of influence must have run primarily from them to the market rates, though policymakers may in turn react to interbank market conditions in setting the former. Figure 6.2 shows the relationship between various key market and administered rates.

Did certain administered rates form a 'corridor' for market rates, giving policymakers potential control over the lower and upper bounds of interbank market rates? The interest rate on excess reserves certainly seems to have set a floor to interbank rates—'the real "zero interest rate" in the Chinese money market', as an official report put it (Yin 2007, p. 164). No bank had an incentive to lend or purchase bills for a yield lower than that on excess reserves, a perfectly liquid and risk-free asset. Indeed, interbank interest rates did not drop below the excess reserve rate, though short-term rates skimmed along this floor for substantial periods in 2001–2003 and (at least in the case of repo lending and PBC bills) 2005. In March 2005, when the PBC abruptly dropped the excess reserve rate from 1.62 to 0.99%, repo and bill rates promptly followed it down.

This may suggest that the central bank potentially had substantial control over actual interbank rates without even needing to engage in open market operations. But this would depend on other rates staying at the floor, and this was not a viable basis for future policy. When the authorities turned to restraint, raising the floor would have continued to encourage banks to keep passively holding reserves rather than engaging in active liquidity management. Tellingly, the central bank never raised the rate on excess reserves, even when it aimed to tighten from 2005. It wanted to wean the banks from their large reserve buffers and guide interbank rates above the floor.

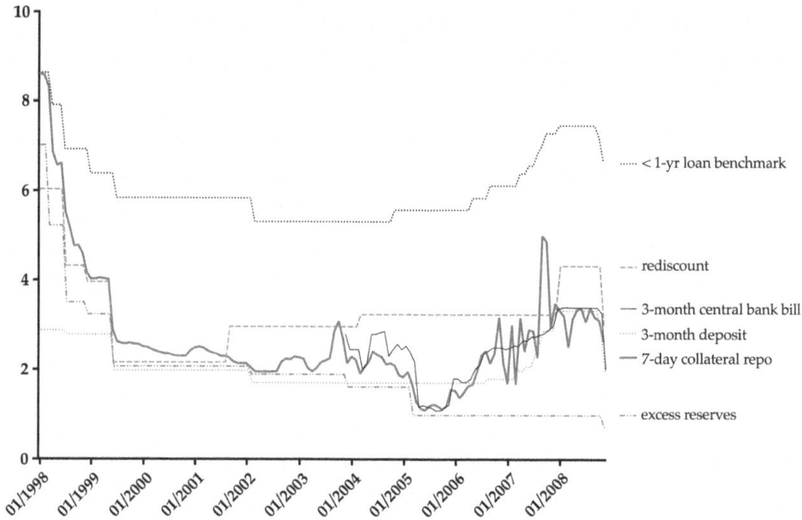

Fig. 6.2 Selected interest rates (*Source* PBC/CEIC)

Whether there was a ceiling to interbank interest rates is more controversial. Xie (2004, p. 20) argues that the PBC lending rate or rediscount rate set an upper limit, but Geiger (2010, pp. 72–73) disagrees. If banks and other financial institutions could freely access central bank funding at a particular rate, this does seem likely to set a ceiling, because none would have an incentive to borrow at higher rates. In practice, interbank rates breached this ceiling in 2003 and 2007, so it was clearly not absolute. The reason is that central bank credit was not available to all financial institutions on demand. It took two forms: outright central bank loans, and the rediscounting of bills. The former were entirely at the discretion of the central bank, and in the 2000s mainly used for two purposes: to subsidise rural credit cooperatives in order to direct credit towards targeted rural areas (PBC 2005a, b, 2007b, 2008); and to support the restructuring of non-performing loans of large state banks, as when the PBC lent large sums in 2005 to asset management companies set up to take these assets onto their balance sheet (Geiger 2010, p. 93; Walter and Howie 2012, pp. 73–76). We do not know the precise amount of direct central bank lending, because it is not separated out from other claims on financial institutions on the central bank's balance sheet (Forssbaeck and Oxelheim 2007, p. 27). It was substantial, but was not a standing facility accessible at the banks' initiative, so did not set a firm ceiling on interbank rates.

The rediscount facility, on the other hand, *was* accessible at will, at least by banks with discounted commercial bills. Before 2001, the rediscount rate was actually set below other interbank market rates (see Fig. 6.2). Rediscounting was used as an open source of liquidity to the banks in the aftermath of the Asian financial crisis. It was set well below lending rates 'to give commercial banks a comfortable spread, serving as an incentive for them to expand discount and rediscount activities' (Xie 2004, p. 3). This abruptly changed in September 2001, when the authorities increased the rate by almost a percentage point, putting it well above interbank market rates. This transformed something which had been a freely available tap for reserves to more of a last-resort source of funding: it was cheaper for banks in good standing to borrow from one another directly or via repo. Resdiscounting at the PBC plunged from RMB277.8bn in 2001 to RMB24.4bn in 2002. It recovered somewhat in 2003 (to RMB107.5bn) as market rates rose to the rediscount rate, but fell back as rates receded, and was only RMB2.5bn in 2005 (Yin 2007, p. 188). It became too small to have an appreciable impact on the monetary base, and was mainly of local importance to the commercial paper market. While it may still have capped the cost of liquidity for banks holding commercial bills, interbank rates sometimes breached it because it was accessible only to institutions with bills to rediscount. So interbank market rates had a floor in the rate on excess reserves, but no definite ceiling.

What role was played by bank lending and deposit rates, also administered? Studies coming out of the Freixas-Rochet 'industrial organisation' tradition (see Sect. 4.3 above) suggest that causality ran from administered deposit and/or loan rates to interbank market rates (Porter and Xu 2009, 2016; He and Wang 2012; Chen et al. 2013). Unlike the typical textbook transmission of policy from interbank rates to longer rates, in China 'a reverse transmission of policy from the retail interest rates to the wholesale money market occurs' (Chen et al. 2013, p. 33). Changes in administered interest rates induce banks, non-bank financial institutions, and non-financial units to adjust their portfolios, which involves shifting their supply/demand functions in the interbank market.

We have criticised this type of model in Sect. 5.1 above. They assume banks were competitive and continuously optimised their balance sheets to a degree we do not believe applies in China in this period. But we do not necessarily disagree with the idea that administered rate adjustments would have some influence on interbank rates. However, the studies do not agree on the nature of this influence. For example, Chen et al. (2013, pp. 55–56), and Porter and Xu (2016, p. 157) suggest that increasing deposit rates lowers interbank rates, because they attract more funds into the banking system from depositors. What the depositors are exchanging for the deposits is left unclear. Conversely, He and Wang (2012, p. 935) posit that increasing deposit rates induces a *rise* in interbank rates. The shift into bank deposits is a shift *out* of non-bank financial institutions, who must in turn reduce their lending into the interbank market. Banks will not make up for this because some proportion of their increase in deposits will be frozen in required reserves, and so not available for lending on the interbank market.

He and Wang (2012) and Porter and Xu (2016) each econometrically confirm their contrasting hypotheses. The former find a substantial positive association: 'a 1% change in the benchmark deposit rate, on average, brings about a 0.61% change in money market rates' (He and Wang 2012, p. 939). The latter find a statistically significant—but practically negligible—negative relationship: 'The impact of a 100-basis-point rise in the deposit rate is a 2.1-basis-point fall in the mean interbank rate' (Porter and Xu 2016, p. 170). As with the estimates of money demand functions discussed in Chapter 3, it seems the studies disagree on the size and even the direction of relationships.

This is not the place for a full exploration of the differences between the models. We think the estimates must be taken with a grain of salt in any case. Adjustments in loan and deposit rates were rare between 1999 and mid-2006. Given the radical transformation of the interbank market over this period, the foreign exchange inflow and the sterilisation strategies for dealing with it, it seems unreasonable to expect a stable relationship among the variables. Neither study includes central foreign exchange purchases among the independent variables, despite including open market operations and adjustments to the required reserve ratio—and we have seen above that these instruments were mainly used to sterilise foreign exchange, so to include one without the other is likely to mislead. Finally, most adjustments to loan and deposit rates took place in a limited period of time. Authorities very rarely adjusted bank rates between 2000 and mid-2006, and then repeatedly raised them over an eighteen-month period. This was an unusual time in which policy was working with many instruments in the interbank market at once, and we are sceptical of regression's power to disentangle the influences at work in these circumstances.

As can be seen in Fig. 6.2, interbank rates had no clear relationship with bank rates between 2000 and 2006: the former fluctuated substantially, while the latter were mostly held still. The upward trend in interbank rates from the end of 2005 began at least six months before policymakers began to increase the bank benchmarks, but increases in the latter were eventually greater. It is notable that the rise in deposit rates 2006–2007 was accompanied by *slower* growth in household deposit accumulation (see Table 2.2)—against the prediction of the basic industrial organisation model. This had much to do with the stock market boom, as we discuss in the next chapter. The rise in interbank rates *relative* to deposit rates, at least early on, may also be part of the explanation: this opened opportunities for non-bank financial institutions to attract funds and invest them on the interbank market. But the effect of such a shift on deposits as a whole is ambiguous, since deposits are reduced in the aggregate only by transactions that cancel them. When households shift funds to non-bank financial institutions, at first this transfers deposits to these units rather than cancelling them. Ultimately, the effect on the stock of deposits depends on extent to which these institutions directly or indirectly extend new finance to government and banks, or facilitate the repayment of bank credit. Later, in 2008, deposit rates rose faster than interbank rates, and deposits again dominated household financial asset accumulation.

References

Bell, Stephen, and Hui Feng. 2013. *The rise of the People's Bank of China: The politics of institutional change.* Cambridge, MA: Harvard University Press.

Burger, Albert E., and Robert H. Rasche. 1977. "Revision of the monetary base." *Federal Reserve Bank of St Louis Review*, July, pp. 13–28.

Chen, Hongyi, Qianying Chen, and Stefan Gerlach. 2013. "The implementation of monetary policy in China: The interbank market and bank lending." In Bang Nam Jeon, and María Pía Olivero (eds.). *Global banking, financial markets and crises*, pp. 31–69. Bingley: Emerald Group Publishing.

Forssbaeck, Jens, and Lars Oxelheim. 2007. "The transition to market-based monetary policy: What can China learn from the European experience?" *Journal of Asian Economics* 18, pp. 257–283.

Gabor, Tamas. 2012. "China's monetary sterilisation and its economical relationship with the European Union." *Crisis Aftermath: Economic policy changes in the EU and its member states*, International Conference Proceedings, pp. 356–381. Available at https://ssrn.com/abstract=2159944. 16 April 2019.

Geiger, Michael. 2008. "Instruments of monetary policy in China and their effectiveness: 1994–2006." UNCTAD Discussion Paper 2008 (2).

Geiger, Michael. 2010. *Monetary policy in China: Institutions, targets, instruments and strategies.* Dissertation, Bayerischen Julius-Maximillians-Universistat Wurzburg.

Girardin, Eric, Sandrine Lunven, and Guonan Ma. 2017. "China's evolving monetary policy rule: From inflation-accommodating to anti-inflation policy." Bank for International Settlements Working Papers 641.

Godley, Wynne, and Marc Lavoie. 2007. *Monetary economics: An integrated approach the credit, money, income, production and wealth.* Houndmills: Palgrave Macmillan.

Green, Stephen. 2005. "Making monetary policy work in China: A report from the money market front line." Stanford Center for International Development Working Paper 245.

He, Dong, and Honglin Wang. 2012. "Dual-track interest rates and the conduct of monetary policy in China." *China Economic Review* 23, pp. 928–947.

Lardy, Nicholas R. 2008. "Financial repression in China." Peterson Institute Policy Brief PB08.

Lavoie, Marc, and Peng Wang. 2012. "The 'compensation' thesis, as exemplified by the case of the Chinese central bank." *International Review of Applied Economics* 26 (3), pp. 287–301.

Li, Qing, Weiqiang Ye, and Yuqing Feng. 2007. Cures for China's feverish stock market. *Caijing English Newsletter*, 11 June.

Ma, Guonan, Yan Xiandong, and Liu Xi. 2011. "China's evolving reserve requirements." BIS Working Papers 360.

Michell, Jo. 2012. *Credit and investment in China: A flow-of-funds analysis.* PhD thesis, SOAS, University of London.

People's Bank of China. 2004. *Monetary Policy Report, Quarter 1.* Beijing: People's Bank of China.

People's Bank of China. 2005a. *Monetary Policy Report, Quarter 2.* Beijing: People's Bank of China.

People's Bank of China. 2005b. *Monetary Policy Report, Quarter 4.* Beijing: People's Bank of China.

People's Bank of China. 2006a. *Monetary Policy Report, Quarter 2.* Beijing: People's Bank of China.

People's Bank of China. 2006b. *Monetary Policy Report, Quarter 3.* Beijing: People's Bank of China.

People's Bank of China. 2007a. *Monetary Policy Report, Quarter 1*. Beijing: People's Bank of China.

People's Bank of China. 2007b. *Monetary Policy Report, Quarter 4*. Beijing: People's Bank of China.

People's Bank of China. 2008. *Monetary Policy Report, Quarter 2*. Beijing: People's Bank of China.

Porter, Nathan, and TengTeng Xu. 2009. "What drives China's interbank market?" IMF Working Paper 09/189.

Porter, Nathan, and TengTeng Xu. 2016. "Money-market rates and retail interest regulation in China: The disconnect between interbank and retail credit conditions." *International Journal of Central Banking* 12 (1), pp. 143–198.

Prasad, Eswar. 2008. "Monetary policy independence, the currency regime, and the capital account in China." In Morris Goldstein and Nicholas R. Lardy (eds.). *Debating China's exchange rate policy*, pp. 77–92. Washington, DC: Peterson Institute for International Economics.

Shu, Chang, and Brian Ng. 2010. "Monetary stance and policy objectives in China." *Hong Kong Monetary Authority China Economic Issues* 1/10.

Stigum, Marcia, and Anthony Crescenzi. 2007. *Stigum's money market*. New York: McGraw-Hill.

Sun, Guofeng. 2015. *Reforms in China's monetary policy: A frontbencher's perspective*. New York: Palgrave Macmillan.

Walter, Carl E., and Fraser J. T. Howie. 2012. *Red capitalism: The fragile financial foundation of China's extraordinary rise*, 2nd ed. Singapore: Wiley.

Xie, Ping. 2004. "China's monetary policy: 1998–2002." Stanford Center for International Development Working Paper 217.

Yin, Jianfeng. 2007. The banking industry. In Yang Li (ed.). *China's banking & financial markets: The internal research report of the Chinese government*, pp. 161–190. Singapore: Wiley.

CHAPTER 7

Instruments II: The Evolution of Policy Strategy

Abstract This is the second of a pair of chapters discussing how Chinese monetary policymakers deployed the instruments they had in the 2000s, and how their strategy evolved. Here we first look at policy strategy for influencing the interbank market. We argue that policy control here was limited by the structural liquidity surplus discussed in the previous chapter, as well as by the fact that many Chinese banks did not tend to continuously optimise their reserve holdings, making demand for reserves unpredictable. The People's Bank of China could use open market operations to influence and smooth market rates, but not control them outright. The lack of control over market rates, as well as uncertainty about transmission from interbank market conditions to bank lending behaviour, forced authorities to rely more heavily on direct banking controls to restrain credit and money expansion.

Keywords Monetary policy · China · Liquidity · Central banking · Interbank market · Transmission · Banking controls

We established in the previous chapter that administered rates—including bank deposit and loan rate benchmarks and limits, the rediscount rate and the rate paid on excess reserves—may have interacted with interbank market rates, but did not tightly constrain them. There was plenty of room for interbank rates to move independently of the administered rates. In this chapter we examine policy strategy for influencing market

M. Beggs and L. Deer, *Remaking Monetary Policy in China*,
https://doi.org/10.1007/978-981-13-9726-4_7

rates, and show that while the central bank increased its capability for open market operations over our period, these remained too weak to be the major policy instrument. Thus the central bank depended on direct requests to the commercial banks to restrain their lending.

7.1 Influencing the Interbank Market

In Sect. 5.2 we discussed the views of PBC economist Sun (2015 [2004]) on the determination of interbank market interest rates. His starting point was a model of supply and demand for excess reserves. But he emphasised that, as of the mid-2000s, Chinese banks did not tend to continuously optimise their reserve holdings. Many allowed reserves to rise and fall relatively passively, within limits. This buffer stock reserve adjustment meant that the supply of reserves did not meet a stable schedule of demand relating the quantity of reserves banks held to interbank interest rates. The standard textbook depiction of open market operations, in which any particular volume of reserves would be associated with a particular interest rate, given the demand schedule, did not apply. When it engaged in an open market operation, the central bank was transacting only with the subset of banks seeking to adjust their liquidity at that time—including both more active managers and others who happened to have reached an adjustment decision point. The demand for reserves/securities on the part of this subset was distinct from the hypothetical overall aggregate demand from all financial institutions if they were all optimising rather than 'satisficing' their reserve holdings. Policymakers could not predict with much confidence what interest rate would be associated with any particular quantity of reserves.

In the textbook view, to target a given interest rate was also to target a particular quantity of reserves. This was not the case for Chinese authorities. Both quantities and interest rates were relevant to their aims, so they sought to manage both, but the targets interacted unpredictably. They could structure open market operations (whether involving repos or bills) in either of two ways: set a price (and so yield) and let demand determine the quantity; or decide on a quantity and let the price (yield) adjust until demand absorbed it. Both bidding processes were used at different times. Until 2003, the PBC preferred to establish the interest rate and let banks decide quantity. When it then became preoccupied with sterilising foreign exchange purchases, this changed.

In either case, the market outcome provided information to the central bank that would feed into later operations and other policy actions.

The fact that operations invited bids on price for a predetermined quantity did not mean policymakers were committed to rigid quantity targets over a longer time horizon. With open market operations taking place once or (after 2003) twice a week, plans for the next one could take into account the outcome of previous rounds. For example, if authorities worried that yields were getting too high they could cut back the quantity of bills offered in later operations, or even switch to fixed-price quantity tenders to stabilise rates—as they did in late 2003 (Yin 2007, pp. 178–179). But the central bank had limited power to simultaneously control both reserve quantities and interbank interest rates. So long as operations were driven mainly by a desire to sterilise the quantity effect of foreign exchange inflows, the PBC had to prioritise the former. The use of reserve requirement hikes and special bills to do the heavy lifting on the quantity front from 2006 freed open market operations to focus on smoothing and guiding interest rates—but this still did not mean tight control, because demand remained somewhat unpredictable.

For much of the period rates hovered around the floor set by the rate paid on excess reserves, because of the abundance of reserves due to foreign exchange purchases. Through 2002, with recovery from the Asian financial crisis underway, the PBC was still eager to keep interbank rates low and stable, even as its open market operations turned to withdrawing reserves in response to foreign exchange inflow (see Sect. 6.1). When rates began to climb at the end of that year, the PBC temporarily switched its open market operations from interest rate bidding to fixed-rate quantity bidding, and successfully capped the rise (Sun 2015 [2003], pp. 135–136).

The following year demonstrated the complexity of the PBC's activity in the interbank market—and of the problems it dealt with. Sterilisation of foreign exchange purchases dominated policy in 2003 (see Fig. 6.1), which meant a primary focus on the quantity of reserves. When central bank bill auctions began in May, the PBC tended to offer fixed quantities and let demand determine price (Geiger 2010, pp. 84–85). But the authorities could not be indifferent to the sharp rise in interbank rates from August. The quantities of bills the Bank wished to sell could be absorbed by the market only at higher yields, but, as mentioned in Sect. 6.1, higher yields risked exacerbating foreign exchange inflow. This was part of the reason authorities turned to a sharp 1-percentage-point hike in the required reserve ratio in August as an alternative means of sterilisation. But in spite of the foreign exchange inflow, this left some small and medium-sized commercial banks short of reserves (PBC 2003, pp. 52–53), adding to demand on the interbank market even as a spate of large listings on the stock exchange raised demand pressure further (Yin 2007, p. 178). By October the 7-day repo rate exceeded 3%, more than a full percentage point higher than it had been in April, and rates oscillated with severe volatility.[1]

This experience demonstrated that reserves could be abundant among banks as a whole, while some faced a shortage, supporting the idea that reserves could sit idle in buffer stocks without being offered for supply on the market. Even while using open market operations to restore liquidity, the PBC complained that bank loans were growing 'faster than desired' (PBC 2003, p. 44): Policy was torn between restraining credit and maintaining market stability. Liquid banks could expand regardless of interbank market rates, and the PBC could not drain them of their spare reserves without causing serious trouble for the less liquid banks.

Again the central bank switched temporarily to fixed-rate quantity bidding (i.e., offering bills at a set rate and allowing buyers to determine the quantity issued), as it lowered the rate on excess reserves in December. Rates on three-month bills, 7-day repos and 7-day interbank loans were all back below 2% by March, but it is unclear how much this was due to bill and reserve interest rate changes, how much to the increased supply of free reserves, and how much to the passing of conditions that had led to high demand for reserves.

The year 2004 saw a refinement of the PBC's sterilisation strategy (Green 2005, p. 19) and a shift in policy intent to stronger restraint, as the consumer price inflation rate rose above 3%. In March, the PBC stated worries about the pace of money and credit growth and announced that 'money and credit growth should be properly controlled' (quoted in Sun 2013, p. 63). Interest rates played a supporting role at best. The bank loan rate benchmarks were not increased until October, and then only by 0.27 percentage points. Bills on issue tripled over the year, and the Bank increased the required reserve ratio by half a percentage point in April.[2]

[1]On 4 November it peaked at 3.64%. (Fig. 6.2 shows the monthly average repo rate so misses the peak and the high day-to-day volatility in this period.)

[2]Note that the construction of Fig. 6.1 may make the timing of policy appear delayed. It presents year-on-year change in each variable. A large upward jump in the PBC's net domestic assets at the very end of 2003 means that it takes some time for the rapid decrease in 2004 to show up in year-on-year change.

The full range of interbank market instruments was now in place—administered rates, central bank bills, and required reserve ratio adjustments—and authorities were developing experience in timing their interventions. But central bank statements reveal that policymakers did not feel they had tight control over interbank market rates. Its operations focused on maintaining market stability by *smoothing* movements in rates and the quantity of free reserves. It worked to offset both movements in foreign exchange reserves and shifts in demand for reserves.

Describing its operations in the first quarter of 2005, the PBC reported that it first responded to an expected seasonal high demand for reserves around New Year and the Spring Festival by 'smooth[ing] the fluctuations of liquidity in the banking system through timely rescheduling the maturity of central bank bills, pre-issuance of central bank bills and conduct of reverse repo operations on a small scale'. With 'abundant liquidity' after the Festival, policy reversed by issuing bills and cutting the rate paid on excess reserves 'to expand the room for money market interest rate movement' (PBC 2005a, p. 10). Note that the PBC did not claim the ability to control rates, but only to 'expand the room' for movement. It seemed to want to foster stability in order to encourage banks to engage more with the market, to make market-based policy more effective *in the future.* Its current operations 'further promoted the market-based interest rate reform and enhanced asset and liability management of commercial banks' (PBC 2005a, p. 10).

Market rates remained low until the end of the year, and PBC statements on open market operations continued to emphasise the aim of reducing volatility (PBC 2005b, p. 12; 2005c, p. 13; 2005d, p. 10). Policy also sought to influence the level of rates, but this was presented as a matter of policy *influence* rather than *control*: for example, in the middle of the year the Bank 'scaled down its sterilisation through open market operations *in an effort to* maintain generally sufficient liquidity in the banking system and to keep the money market interest rate low' (PBC 2005c, p. 13, emphasis added). It '*allowed* the market interest rate to move slightly downward' (PBC 2005d, p. 10, emphasis added). It took some credit for the rise in rates at the end of 2005, but claimed to have 'reasonably pushed the money market rate upward', not to have set it (PBC 2005d, p. 10). Policy in the interbank market was mainly a matter of leaning with or against movements in the market, and the PBC did not claim tight control. Any too-strong attempt to direct rates by withdrawing or freezing reserves risked repeating the volatility of late 2003.

Equities became a major additional source of instability for the interbank market between 2006 and 2008, forcing authorities to continue to prioritise the smoothing of volatility. We argued in Sect. 2.3 that equities were the main alternative to deposits as a store of value for households. It is clear from Tables 2.1 and 2.2 that the sharemarket boom of 2006–2008 had a major impact on household balance sheets. Household wealth flowed into equities, and this combined with the market's enormous rise greatly increased their share of household financial assets: from 3.8% in 2005 to 15.4% in 2007, falling back to 5.9% as values retreated in 2008. The Shanghai Stock Exchange Composite Index rose from 1181 at the beginning of 2006 to a peak of 4335 in May 2007, before falling back to 1954 by the end of 2008. Market turnover rose and fall with the price index, with much more amplitude. Earlier in the decade, daily stock turnover on the exchange was typically below RMB5bn, and it rarely rose above RMB20bn; in 2007 it spiked as high as RMB271bn, and the daily average that year was RMB126bn.

From the perspective of the banking system, this trading took place among its customers. Whether equities were sold from firms to households, or between households, it involved a *transfer* of deposits. (The unusually small flow into deposits by households in 2007 has a counterpart in an unusually large flow by firms [see Table 2.3].) But the enormous rise in turnover would have had its counterpart within the banking system as the banks cleared with one another, and it is no accident that this was a particularly volatile time for interbank interest rates. Initial public offerings were especially important, because they involved a 'lock-up' of large amounts of funds for around a week. He and Wang (2012, p. 939) note that funds locked up in this way could be much larger in value than the typical central bank bill issuance, and there was a wave of IPOs coinciding with the period of rate volatility 2006–2007 (which was also of course the period of high stockmarket turnover). Both He and Wang (2012) and Porter and Xu (2016) include IPO amounts in their models of interbank rates. The former find them significant but not of much importance in explaining changes in rates; the latter find them insignificant in explaining the average level of rates, but significant in explaining volatility.

Porter and Xu (2016, p. 171) speculate that the value of IPOs possibly had little impact on the level of interbank rates because of 'offsetting policy actions'. This points to the inherent difficulty of disentangling causation around interbank rates—not just with respect to IPOs, but more generally—when policy is being deliberately adjusted to counter and smooth the effect of exogenous influences.

The PBC's own statements suggest that its open market operations in this period continued to aim more at moderating volatility and smoothing rates than at setting their level. As rates rose slowly but steadily across 2006, the Bank presented itself as *allowing* or *guiding* (PBC 2006a, p. 11) rather than *setting* them upward. In China there was still no equivalent to the US federal funds rate, which the central bank could control and be confident in its pass-through to other money market rates. The PBC presented itself as a market participant with special powers, rather than an institution capable of determining rates at will: 'market interest rates played a role in adjusting fund supply and demand' (PBC 2006d, p. 11). Of course, its bill sales and required reserve ratio hikes were important on the supply side, and overall, this was a rare time in which authorities withdrew more liquidity from the banks than foreign exchange purchases provided (see Fig. 6.1). If the authorities had objected to the rising rates, they could have allowed more free reserves to remain in the system. But the Bank did not appear confident of its ability to control any rate with precision, because of (1) the difficulty in predicting market demand for reserves, (2) the tension between its quantity (sterilisation) and rate aims, and (3) its desire to avoid the extreme volatility that came with tightness in the money market. Volatility risked transmitting instability into the banking system and then to the rest of the economy, and discouraged bank reliance on the market, undermining the basis for more effective market-based policy in the future.

As initial public offerings began to absorb reserves in mid-2006, the PBC found the rates at which its desired quantity of bills could be sold began to rise rapidly, alongside the rates on substitutes—repos and unsecured interbank loans. Worried about the liquidity of some institutions, in August the authorities switched again briefly to fixed-rate quantity bidding on 1-year bills in an attempt to stabilise rates, while adjusting deposit and loan rates upward. It claimed some success: the rise in rates was halted and partially reversed for a few months, not only for bills but for money market instruments in general (PBC 2006c, p. 14). The Bank continued a pattern of 'flexibly switch[ing] between price bidding and quantity bidding' (PBC 2006d, p. 11) and was able to keep its bill yields relatively stable, climbing moderately, over the following year.

These were the circumstances in which policy settled into the dual strategy of using changes in the required reserve ratio (and mandatory 'special bills') to 'deeply freeze' the bulk of reserves created by foreign exchange inflow, now at its peak, carving out space to use open market operations for more delicate fine-tuning (see Fig. 6.1). We are now in a position to see the outcome. PBC statements in 2007 and early 2008 repeatedly discuss interbank market policy in terms of both sterilisation and stabilisation. The former involved the overall draining of liquidity with less frequent but large scale shifts in reserve requirements. The latter involved open market operations sometimes removing further reserves and sometimes injecting them back into the system, often with special attention to stabilising rates at particular points in the maturity structure (e.g., PBC 2007a, pp. 15–16; 2007b, p. 10; 2007c, p. 9; 2008a, p. 11; 2008b, p. 12). But though the Bank was successful in stabilising yields on its own bills, it was much less so in stabilising short-term interbank rates. Seven-day repo and interbank loan rates fluctuated widely for all of 2007 and spiked dramatically at the end of that year (see Fig. 6.1).

The goal of a 'market-based' policy centred on operations in the interbank market remained an aspiration for the future rather than a reliable basis for effective policy in the present. Policymakers paid a lot of attention to the interbank market, but saw it as a work in progress. Turnover grew enormously between 2006 and 2008 (see Table 2.5), and there was reasonable hope that it would mature into a workable arena for transmitting policy impulses towards credit and money targets. But this would depend on more widespread use of the market for bank liquidity management, so that its rates would truly represent the marginal cost of liquidity, and this in turn depended on the further erosion of bank free reserve buffers. The PBC continued to develop the institutional infrastructure of the market, for example by leading the development of a publicly quoted 'Shibor' set of benchmark interbank lending rates, which debuted in 2007 (PBC 2007d, pp. 22–24). But in spite of the vastly increased volume of transactions, the interbank market remained very volatile. Though medium-term rates were fairly stable in 2007, it was not uncommon for short-term interbank rates to suddenly leap or fall several percentage points: the Shibor benchmark 7-day rate spiked by more than a percentage point twelve times that year, including a five-percentage-point leap in September and an eight-percentage-point leap in October (PBC 2007d, p. 24). So long as such jumps were routine, it was risky for institutions to rely on the market for liquidity.

Finally, we should also recognise that an opposition between 'controls' and 'market-based' policy is problematic for China. The ability to use open market operations for fine-tuning liquidity and targeting interest rates depended on the use of reserve requirements to do the heavy-duty work of sterilising the impact of foreign exchange intervention—at least as long as the central bank was committed to managing the exchange rate, 'market-based policy' fundamentally depended on controls.

7.2 Last Resort: Window Guidance

In the previous section we established that Chinese authorities did not have precise control over interbank market interest rates in the 2000s. Even if they had, however, this would not have been sufficient for a market-based transmission mechanism, as there was a loose relationship between interbank market conditions and bank lending.

In 2006 the PBC acknowledged that it was still some way off from being able to control its targets simply by managing the interbank market. On the one hand, it emphasised the distance policy had come over the last decade: 'With monetary policy transformed from direct control to indirect management, liquidity management increasingly has become a key component in the implementation of the central bank's monetary policy' (PBC 2006b, p. 6). On the other hand, it urged observers to recognise that there was no tight relationship between bank liquidity and ultimate policy targets:

> Since the day-to-day management of banking liquidity by the central bank is not directly related to the level of the economic variables, such as fixed-asset investment growth, it is inappropriate to conclude that liquidity should be tightened or loosened simply based on a temporary volatility in investment growth. In general, the interaction and causality between liquidity and various economic variables need to be carefully studied and prudently judged. (PBC 2006b, p. 6)

It had already been clear by 2003 that open market operations would not be enough to control lending (Green 2005, p. 10; Forssbaeck and Oxelheim 2007, p. 278). In 2002 and 2003, the pace of loan growth (and, to a lesser extent M2 growth) substantially exceeded the target, as shown in Table 7.1. The excess reserve-deposit ratio across all depository institutions trended downward substantially (see Fig. 4.2). Banks were running down their ample reserve buffers to increase lending, and policymakers feared that moderate inflation would pick up speed.

Table 7.1 Money and loan growth: targets and actual; CPI inflation (%)

	M2: target	*M2: actual*	*Loans: target*	*Loans: actual*	*CPI inflation: actual*
1998	16–18	14.8	12.7	15.5	−1.0
1999	14–15	14.7	15.7	8.3	−1.0
2000	14–15	15.4	11.7	6.0	1.5
2001	15–16	14.4	13.1	13.0	−0.3
2002	13	16.9	11.6	16.9	−0.4
2003	16	19.6	13.7	21.1	3.2
2004	17	14.9	16.4	12.1	2.4
2005	15	16.3	14.1	9.3	1.6
2006	14	17.0	12.8	15.7	2.8
2007	16	16.7	No target announced	16.1	6.5
2008	16	17.8	No target announced	15.9	1.2

Note We have used Geiger's calculations for loan target growth, and official PBC data from the CEIC database for actual growth rates. The actual growth rates reported by Geiger usually but do not always match the numbers in the database, perhaps because these were revised after the reports from which Geiger drew his data

Source Geiger (2010, pp. 112, 120); PBC/CEIC; National Bureau of Statistics/CEIC

While central bankers might look forward to a future in which they had more control over money market conditions, and in which money market conditions had more influence on bank lending, they needed effective policy instruments in the meantime. In early June 2003, the PBC issued a notice calling on banks to restrict credit for real estate. It then held a series of meetings with banks later in the year calling for general restraint—framed in terms of capital adequacy, loan-deposit and liquidity ratios (PBC 2003, pp. 55–56). This developed into an ongoing schedule of conferences and monthly assessments in which the PBC delivered such 'window guidance' requests to banks (Geiger 2010, pp. 88–92).

Just a few years after abandoning the Credit Plan, policymakers had returned to direct influence on bank lending. This cut through both the uncertainties facing market-based policy: slippages in the central bank's control of interbank market conditions, and slippages between those conditions and bank lending behaviour. It acted directly on the last. But with it came another uncertainty: How closely would the guidance be followed?

Window guidance came somewhere between enforceable directives and moral suasion. In practice, requests were delivered in scheduled conferences and meetings, as well as in regular written assessments delivered by the central bank. The instructions varied in specificity and force. Though they were not legally binding, they had power for two reasons. First, much of the banking system remained state-owned and monetary authorities had organisational superiority over the leadership of the large banks: The PBC governor outranked the heads of the big state banks within the Communist Party, and both the PBC and the China Banking Regulatory Commission had power over senior appointments at the banks (Geiger 2010, p. 88; Chen et al. 2013, p. 36). Second, the central bank had the power to penalise non-cooperation, for example by issuing special central bank bills on a mandatory basis to recalcitrant banks (PBC 2007a, p. 16).

Window guidance is not easy to measure because it is not transparent. Not only do we not know how faithfully the banks complied with the central bank's requests, we do not now in any detail the content of the requests themselves. Until 2008, the PBC did report the general shape of the guidance in its quarterly policy reports, and we get some sense of the degree of urgency from these descriptions, but they remain vague.[3] In 2008 the PBC temporarily stopped reporting window guidance—likely because of international criticism of direct controls as means of policy—but continued to rely on it all the same (Geiger 2010, p. 92).

[3]For example, the Monetary Policy Report for Quarter One, 2005, describes window guidance as follows: 'Window guidance of the central bank will be improved to further strengthen coordination between credit policies and industrial policies and timely convey the policy intentions to the financial institutions. The commercial banks are encouraged to take preemptive measures to respond to cyclical development and industrial changes, strengthen their ability to judge market risks, improve risk control and further transform their operating mechanisms. The loan granting and approval procedures will be reformed based on market principles, and the risk management system will be improved. The commercial banks will be encouraged to continue adopting different loan policies to different sectors and enterprises. In particular, working capital loans will be timely provided to the enterprises with marketable products and good profitability and those contributing to job creation. Credit support will be strengthened to promote the development of agriculture, small- and medium-sized enterprises, consumer spending, employment and education. Policy guidance on consumer credit will be enhanced, and the commercial banks will be encouraged to improve their financial services to the non-state sector. Developments of the housing market will be closely monitored and various policies be coordinated to ensure the healthy development of the housing market' (PBC 2005a, p. 38).

Nevertheless, Delatte (2008), Chen et al. (2017), and Angrick and Yoshino (2018) have made valiant efforts to measure window guidance. Delatte (2008, pp. 12, 16) uses the PBC's Monetary Policy Reports and some secondary literature to assess the policy stance in each quarter as either 'easy' or 'tight'. Within the period of interest to us, 1998Q1–2002Q4 is coded as 'easy' and 2003Q1–2007Q1 (the end of her series) as 'tight'. Chen et al. (2017) and Angrick and Yoshino (2018) use textual analysis of the PBC's Monetary Policy Reports and, in the latter case, Monetary Policy Committee meeting notes, to classify the strength and direction of window guidance policy for each quarter on a five-point scale from −2 (most restrictive) to +2 (most encouraging), with 0 representing neutral or no window guidance. Chen et al. (2017, pp. 40–41) break the years between 2000 and 2009 into five discrete periods for window guidance:

- 2000Q1–2002Q4: macroeconomically neutral (with some sectoral direction)
- 2003Q1–2004Q4: strongly restrictive
- 2005Q1–2006Q1: moderately restrictive
- 2006Q2–2008Q2: strongly restrictive
- 2008Q3–2009Q1: strongly encouraging

Angrick and Yoshino's (2018, pp. 41–42) classifications are more finely grained—i.e., show more variation in window guidance from quarter to quarter—but do not differ in the basic pattern: strong restraint 2003–2004, more moderate restraint 2005–2006, strengthening again 2006–2008.

These classifications represent policymakers' intent, at least as expressed publicly, but what of the effectiveness? Delatte (2008) concludes that window guidance had only a limited impact on credit growth. She estimates a single model of credit supply for the whole period 1986Q1–2007Q1, finding no structural break even following policy reform around 1998. She measures the impact of window guidance by including a dummy variable in the model representing policy stance and estimating its impact on the relationship between excess reserves and bank credit. The model also includes the spread between bank lending and deposit rates, but this is found to be not significant. She therefore concludes that 'administrative control is the only determinant of the credit supply in China', but that this control has only limited effect: 'tight' policy reduced credit by only 15% from what it would otherwise be (Delatte 2008, p. 21). This must however be seen as a tentative result. It presumes equal reliance on window guidance in all periods of 'tight' policy, and uniform application in periods of tightness. Geiger (2010, p. 152) suggests that Delatte's measure 'may well understate the importance of window guidance'.

Chen et al. (2017) and Angrick and Yoshino (2018) both find window guidance to have a substantial effect on credit growth. The former find that strongly restrictive window guidance was followed by 'sharp declines' in the growth rates of new lending and the loan-GDP ratio, while moderately restrictive window guidance stabilised these growth rates (Chen et al. 2017, p. 11). Over the whole 2000–2016 period in their study, they find a correlation of 0.29 between the window guidance variable (again, ranging from −2 [strongly restrictive] to +2 [strongly encouraging]) and total loan growth, and a correlation of 0.36 between the variable and loans to non-financial sectors (Chen et al. 2017, p. 10).[4]

Angrick and Yoshino (2018) use a structural vector autoregression model to estimate the effect on bank credit growth of window guidance alongside changes in reserve requirements, bank interest rates, the discount rate, and the overnight interbank rate. They study the whole period 2000–2017, but find a structural break in November 2008 with the impact of the global financial crisis. They therefore present estimates for pre- and post-crisis policy transmission, and the earlier period coincides well with our period of interest. For this pre-crisis period, they find that changes in the required reserve ratio, in the interbank overnight rate, and in the central bank's discount rate are not significant in predicting bank credit growth.[5] A shift in the stance of window guidance, on

[4] Of course this correlation is not in itself strong evidence for the effectiveness of window guidance. Unlike the two other studies we discuss here, Chen et al. (2017) do not focus on econometric estimation. Instead, the authors develop a DSGE model of the Chinese banking system and economy and use it to simulate the effects of window guidance reactions to various shocks. They calibrate the model mostly with average data from the 2010s, and are mostly concerned with the effectiveness of window guidance in stimulating rather than restraining lending.

[5] We focus here on the model incorporating narrative measures of the 'narrow' indicator, i.e., the indicator based on Angrick and Yoshino's assessments of policy statements specifically related to window guidance. Conclusions from the other models are not substantially different. We report significance here based on the authors' 95% confidence bands.

the other hand, was significant and associated with a substantial change in the pace of credit growth. A one-point shift in the stance of window guidance towards restraint (e.g., from 'neutral' to 'moderately restrictive' or from 'moderately' to 'strongly restrictive') was associated with a cumulative five-percentage-point decline in the rate of credit growth within a year, other factors being equal. The apparent impact of shifts in bank interest rates was more uncertain but also significant and positive, with a one-percentage-point hike in the average retail rate associated with a similar decline in the rate of credit growth (Angrick and Yoshino 2018, pp. 21–27).[6]

It is possible these results underestimate the importance of bank liquidity (spare reserves) on willingness to lend. The failure to find an impact of changes in reserve requirements should not surprise us. As discussed in Sect. 6.1, adjustments to the required reserve ratio were largely aimed at sterilising the effect of foreign exchange purchases on the monetary base. It is the combined impact of ratio adjustments and other influences on bank excess reserves that matter, but these other influences are not in Angrick and Yoshino's model. So it is possible that some of the influence they attribute to window guidance is related to changes in bank liquidity. Conversely, Delatte's (2008) model tests the effect of window guidance by estimating the difference it makes to credit growth at a given quantity of excess reserves, so does not consider the effectiveness of bank controls considered more broadly, i.e., including the influence of reserve requirements on excess reserves.

In any case, there is no doubt that restrictive policy depended fundamentally on direct banking controls, including window guidance, the required reserve ratio, and the interest rate benchmarks. By mid-decade, policymakers and commentators alike saw direct controls as the essential element of monetary policy (Green 2005, p. 21), and it seemed to be successful. The turn to window guidance in mid-2003 was followed by a dramatic slowdown in loan growth: from a far over-target 21.1% in 2003, it fell to 11.6% in 2004 and 9.8% in 2005 (see Table 7.1). Authorities loosened their requests in 2005, but maintained 'moderate

[6]The estimated response of credit growth to window guidance holds up in the alternative model using an indicator based on statements about policy stance in general, rather than window guidance specifically. But in this alternative model, the impact of bank interest rates is substantially lower and not significant at the 5% level (Angrick and Yoshino 2018, p. 22).

restraint' according to both Chen et al. (2017) and Angrick and Yoshino (2018). The excess reserve-deposit ratio stabilised around 4% (see Fig. 4.2). M2 growth fell for a few months, but then bounced back substantially faster than credit growth in this period, largely due to foreign exchange inflows (see Fig. 4.1).[7] With window guidance restraining loans, banks were shifting their balance sheets towards securities. As discussed in Sect. 7.1, the interbank market was flooded with liquidity, and interbank rates dropped towards the floor of the rate on excess reserves.

This meant the system retained a large potential for expanding lending, and in 2006 this potential began to be actualised. Loan growth jumped upwards in the first few months of the year—year-on-year growth rising from 10% to above 15%, where it remained into 2008. Inflation began to rise to rates not seen for a decade, with consumer price inflation of 6.5% over 2007.

From this point, authorities used the full range of controls together to restrain bank credit: higher reserve requirements, bank interest rate hikes, and intensified window guidance. Beginning in April 2006, benchmark loan rates were increased in eight steps over the next two years, from 5.58 to 7.47% in mid-2008. With the money market flush with liquidity in mid-2005, the spread between the 7-day interbank lending rate and the 1-year loan rate had increased to 4 percentage points. But once bank rates headed upwards, the spread narrowed, as interbank rates tended to follow loan and deposit rates up with the increased pace of lending absorbing excess reserves. Short-term interbank rates were left to be volatile, showing that authorities were not inclined to smooth the market much or accommodate demand for liquidity. The 7-day interbank loan rate temporarily reached as high as 4.75% in September 2007.

Window guidance efforts were redoubled from mid-2006 (Geiger 2010, pp. 90–92; Chen et al. 2017, pp. 40–41; Angrick and Yoshino 2018, pp. 41–42). The central bank convened a number of extraordinary meetings with bank managers, on top of regular monthly assessments. The urgency and force of requests at this time can be read from the PBC's reports: Banks were told 'to comprehensively, correctly, and actively implement the macroeconomic management policies formulated

[7] Even if the PBC sterilised the effect of its foreign exchange purchases on the monetary base by selling bills and increasing the required reserve ratio, this did not in itself sterilise the impact on M2.

by the central government' (PBC 2007a, p. 57; and see PBC 2007b, pp. 10–11, 11–12). The requests continued into 2008, even as the PBC stopped reporting them (Geiger 2010, p. 92). The central bank even revived a regulation that was already on the books but unenforced, capping each bank's loans to non-financial borrowers at 75% to deposits (Hachem and Song 2017, p. 2).

As can be seen from Fig. 4.1 and Table 7.1, loan growth did not reach the frantic pace of 2003, and slowed down in 2008. It is difficult to judge the success of window guidance in this period, because the PBC did not announce credit targets for 2007 or 2008. The 2006 credit target of 12.8% was substantially overshot (15.7%), and authorities surely would have preferred lower credit growth in inflationary 2007. But it did not approach the very high pace of 2003, and window guidance no doubt played a role.

However much authorities may have wished to replace direct controls with 'market-based policy', this was not yet possible in the 2000s. As we detailed in the previous sections in this chapter, there was no reliable transmission mechanism through the interbank market. Policy could not rely on market-based policy, because the chain was broken at three points. They did not have reliable control over interbank rates—certainly not fine control. They could not depend on interbank rates being passed on to bank lending rates. Finally, they were not confident that credit (or the money supply) would be responsive to lending rates. In the absence of these connections, Chinese policy had to revert to direct controls.

References

Angrick, Stefan, and Naoyuki Yoshino. 2018. "From window guidance to interbank rates: Tracing the transition of monetary policy in Japan and China." Bank of Finland Institute for Economies in Transition Discussion Papers 4.

Chen, Hongyi, Qianying Chen, and Stefan Gerlach. 2013. "The implementation of monetary policy in China: The interbank market and bank lending." In Bang Nam Jeon, and María Pía Olivero (eds.). *Global banking, financial markets and crises*, pp. 31–69. Bingley: Emerald Group Publishing.

Chen, Hongyi, Michael Funke, Ivan Lozev, and Andrew Tsang. 2017. "To guide or not to guide? Quantitative monetary policy tools and macroeconomic dynamics in China." Bank of Finland Institute for Economies in Transition Discussion Papers 3.

Delatte, Anne-Laure. 2008. "Monetary policy and macrocontrol in China: The actual impact of window guidance." Unpublished paper. Available at http://citeseerx.ist.psu.edu/viewdoc/download?doi=10.1.1.651.7744&rep=rep1&type=pdf. 15 April 2019.

Forssbaeck, Jens, and Lars Oxelheim. 2007. "The transition to market-based monetary policy: What can China learn from the European experience?" *Journal of Asian Economics* 18, pp. 257–283.

Geiger, Michael. 2010. *Monetary policy in China: Institutions, targets, instruments and strategies.* Dissertation, Bayerischen Julius-Maximillians-Universistat Wurzburg.

Green, Stephen. 2005. "Making monetary policy work in China: A report from the money market front line." Stanford Center for International Development Working Paper 245.

Hachem, Kinda Cheryl, and Zheng Michael Song. 2017. "Liquidity regulation and credit booms: Theory and evidence from China." NBER Working Paper Series 21880.

He, Dong, and Honglin Wang. 2012. "Dual-track interest rates and the conduct of monetary policy in China." *China Economic Review* 23, pp. 928–947.

People's Bank of China. 2003. *Monetary Policy Report, Quarter 3.* Beijing: People's Bank of China.

People's Bank of China. 2005a. *Monetary Policy Report, Quarter 1.* Beijing: People's Bank of China.

People's Bank of China. 2005b. *Monetary Policy Report, Quarter 2.* Beijing: People's Bank of China.

People's Bank of China. 2005c. *Monetary Policy Report, Quarter 3.* Beijing: People's Bank of China.

People's Bank of China. 2005d. *Monetary Policy Report, Quarter 4.* Beijing: People's Bank of China.

People's Bank of China. 2006a. *Monetary Policy Report, Quarter 1.* Beijing: People's Bank of China.

People's Bank of China. 2006b. *Monetary Policy Report, Quarter 2.* Beijing: People's Bank of China.

People's Bank of China. 2006c. *Monetary Policy Report, Quarter 3.* Beijing: People's Bank of China.

People's Bank of China. 2006d. *Monetary Policy Report, Quarter 4.* Beijing: People's Bank of China.

People's Bank of China. 2007a. *Monetary Policy Report, Quarter 1.* Beijing: People's Bank of China.

People's Bank of China. 2007b. *Monetary Policy Report, Quarter 2.* Beijing: People's Bank of China.

People's Bank of China. 2007c. *Monetary Policy Report, Quarter 3.* Beijing: People's Bank of China.

People's Bank of China. 2007d. *Monetary Policy Report, Quarter 4.* Beijing: People's Bank of China.

People's Bank of China. 2008a. *Monetary Policy Report, Quarter 1.* Beijing: People's Bank of China.

People's Bank of China. 2008b. *Monetary Policy Report, Quarter 2.* Beijing: People's Bank of China.

Porter, Nathan, and TengTeng Xu. 2016. "Money-market rates and retail interest regulation in China: The disconnect between interbank and retail credit conditions." *International Journal of Central Banking* 12 (1), pp. 143–198.

Sun, Rongrong. 2013. "Does monetary policy matter in China? A narrative approach." *China Economic Review* 26, pp. 56–74.

Sun, Guofeng. 2015. *Reforms in China's monetary policy: A frontbencher's perspective.* New York: Palgrave Macmillan.

Yin, Jianfeng. 2007. "The banking industry." In Yang Li (ed.). *China's banking & financial markets: The internal research report of the Chinese government*, pp. 161–190. Singapore: Wiley.

CHAPTER 8

Conclusion

Abstract In this final chapter, we review the book's argument as to why Chinese monetary policy leaned so heavily on direct banking controls in the 2000s, and comment on the legacy this period has left in Chinese monetary policy. The emergence of a Chinese form of 'shadow banking' reacted to banking controls, and seemed to undermine policy dependence on such direct measures. In the 2010s, policymakers reconfirmed their intent to deregulate bank interest rates, lower reserve requirements, and build their capacity to manipulate interbank market conditions. It seemed again that Chinese policy was 'liberalising'. But authorities also showed a willingness to extend and intensify regulation over the 'shadow banking' sector, bank loans resurged as the overwhelmingly dominant source of finance, and most of the control-based instruments of the 2000s remain.

Keywords Monetary policy · China · Liquidity · Central banking · Reform

As the US financial crisis intensified and spread around the world in the last half of 2008, Chinese macroeconomic policy was reversed. The PBC later reported that from mid-year it 'reduced the intensity of open market operations, increased the new loan quota for the full year to about 4 trillion, and guided financial institutions to increase credit inputs' (PBC 2008b, p. 10). Later in the year, it

M. Beggs and L. Deer, *Remaking Monetary Policy in China*,
https://doi.org/10.1007/978-981-13-9726-4_8

> sent signals to ensure economic growth and maintain market confidence, cut the benchmark deposit and lending interest rates on five occasions, explicitly lifted the rigid control of aggregate credit planning, ensured sufficient liquidity for the banking system, promoted the reasonable and stable growth of money and credit aggregates, actively supported other economic stimulus policies sponsored by the central government, and strengthened financial support to economic development. (PBC 2008b, p. 10)

At the same time, the government announced an enormous fiscal stimulus package to be delivered by a combination of national and local governments. The years of monetary policy restraint were over, and with them the phase of policy development we have described in this book.

In the final chapter, we first review our argument. Why did Chinese policy in the 2000s lean so heavily on direct banking controls, despite the professed desire to move towards 'market-based' policy? Then in the concluding section we comment on the legacy this period has left in Chinese monetary policy. The emergence of a Chinese form of 'shadow banking' reacted to banking controls, and seemed to undermine policy dependence on such direct measures. In the 2010s policymakers reconfirmed their intent to deregulate bank interest rates, lower reserve requirements, and build their capacity to manipulate interbank market conditions. It seemed again that Chinese policy was 'liberalising'. But authorities also showed a willingness to extend and intensify regulation over the 'shadow banking' sector, bank loans resurged as the overwhelmingly dominant source of finance, and most of the control-based instruments of the 2000s remain.

8.1 Summary

Chinese monetary policy was (and remains) bank-centred first and foremost because the financial system itself was (and remains) bank-dominated, to a degree far surpassing even the 'bank-centred' financial systems of Germany and Japan. As discussed in Chapter 2, bank loans were the main source of finance to the non-financial sector, and their deposits made up the bulk of the financial assets held by non-financial units. Most of the financial system, in other words, was intermediated by bank balance sheets. The absolute dominance of bank loans declined over our period, but banks were still highly involved in alternative forms of finance. Financial markets were growing, but these were themselves dominated by bank trading, to the extent that the main money and bond markets were known as *interbank* markets, their turnover far surpassing the public exchanges. Inevitably, the transmission of policy would run through the commercial banks. The banking system was highly concentrated, with four large state-owned banks holding more than half of total bank assets—leaving the system amenable to direct control.

Unusually, Chinese authorities remained committed to quantitative money and credit targets, long past their abandonment by most Western central banks. Interest rates were not an effective intermediate target in China, because of doubts that investment was responsive to them. Quantitative targets filled the gap. But China was not immune to the problems that had led to the abandonment of monetary targeting elsewhere: instability in the demand for money, and problems in controlling supply. Policymakers did not naively believe in stable demand for money, a stable money multiplier relating monetary base to money stock, or their ability to fully control the base. But the money targets worked as an easily communicated political anchor for tighter policy, and an intermediate target by which to navigate in the absence of anything better. The targets were treated as rough guides rather than as tools for fine-tuning.

Money and credit quantities may make sense as intermediate targets even if they have no tight, predictable relationship to the ultimate targets of investment, output and inflation. Large reserves of idle bank deposits were potential sources of finance for investment: some economists suggested that a 'money overhang' (Gerlach and Kong 2005) or 'money gap' (Burdekin and Siklos 2008)—i.e., money stocks higher than estimates of long-run money-demand—was a good predictor of future inflation, even if 'excess' stocks could persist for some time. Bank credit was important to policy both for its role in financing expenditure directly, and its connection to the money supply. With its financial sector so bank-centred, Chinese policymakers had very good reason to focus on the 'credit channel' of policy transmission.

Transmission through bank balance sheets is not well understood. We argued that neither the traditional money multiplier nor the 'industrial organisation approach' give a good explanation. A stable ratio between monetary base and money stock depends on the stability of the bank reserve-deposit ratio and of the public's currency-deposit ratio. In China, the latter was not constant, declining over the 2000s, but its trend at least was relatively predictable. That of the former, on the other hand, was not: the banking system had large stocks of excess reserves, which fluctuated considerably. Even if the central bank had control over the reserve base (which it did not, not least because of the fixed exchange rate), this was not a reliable fulcrum for controlling the supply of either money or bank credit.

The 'industrial organisation approach' has been a popular framework for understanding the Chinese banking system, but we have argued that it has problems in explaining the nature of the relationship between bank credit and deposit growth. It rightly treats banks as institutions that manage their balance sheets strategically rather than mechanically. But it is misguided in treating the demand for bank credit and the demand for deposits as independent from one another, and neglects the importance of liquidity as a constraint on bank behaviour. It treats banks as facing a supply curve for 'savings' in the deposit market, and a demand curve for credit in the loans market, with the deposit and loan interest rate equilibrating their respective markets. It effectively treats banks as channelling for 'funds' from depositors to borrowers. We quoted PBC economist Sun (2015 [2001], p. 18) rejecting the concept of 'funds' that can be passed between banks and customers, in favour of a conception of banking as 'self-balancing behaviour of… double-entry bookkeeping'.

We elaborated on this understanding of banking and its implications for the transmission of monetary policy. Chinese policymakers saw the money supply as endogenous to the workings of the banking system, but endogenous in the sense that it responded to the demand for credit, not the demand for money. The main bank balance sheet counterparts to money supply growth in the period were expansions in credit, as well as the acquisition of foreign exchange and (to a much lesser extent) government debt by the banking system. Since the exchange rate peg left the PBC little control over its foreign exchange purchases, bank credit was the main potential intermediate influence over deposits, as well as a target in its own right.

The banking system did not need to raise 'funds' from non-bank firms and households before lending, but created deposits when lending. Bank lending affects not only the stock of deposits (as these are connected by bank balance sheets) but also the *demand* for deposits. This is partly because bank credit influences investment and therefore income and the 'equilibrium' demand for money. Also, to the extent that firms and households passively hold a 'buffer stock' of deposits, demand will adapt to supply for a considerable 'disequilibrium' period of time. There are reasons to believe that buffer stock demand for money (Goodhart 1989) was particularly important in China in the 2000s, because of the dearth of alternative financial assets. In any case, a shift in liquidity preference (a desire change the amount of money held at given levels of income and interest rates) had little potential for changing the stock of deposits. Deposits are created or cancelled only through transactions between banks and non-banks, and there were few types of asset exchanged across that boundary in that period in China. Demand for deposits could be brought back into equilibrium with supply through changes in the price of other financial assets, rather than through deposit interest rates. Equities and real estate filled this role as the main alternative stores of value for Chinese households in the mid-2000s.

Instead of deposit-raising, 'the only constraint on lending activities is the requirement to hold reserves' (Sun 2015 [2001], p. 8). A bank could issue a deposit at will, but since deposits are promises to pay reserves, it was limited by its ability to meet this promise and the potential cost of doing so. This constraint worked through the cost and availability of reserves on the interbank market. In theory, interbank market conditions would influence bank lending because the interest rate on borrowed reserves represented the marginal cost of balance sheet expansion. (The deposit rate ceiling largely prevented banks from obtaining reserves by competing for deposits, but they could expand by borrowing directly on the interbank market.)

These rates would—again, in theory—be determined by the equilibrium of supply and demand for reserves. Chinese banks had to meet a required reserve-to-deposit ratio, which could be varied by authorities. They also had to hold at least enough excess reserves on top of this to meet potential reserve outflows, or else be ready to borrow reserves as necessary. Bank liquidity preference involved a trade-off between holding spare low-yielding but safe reserves, and holding higher yielding assets with the risk of having to borrow reserves at potentially high rates to meet unexpected outflows. System-level demand for reserves would therefore be a function of deposits and the interbank rate. Market-based policy rested on the ability of the central bank to influence conditions of reserve supply in response to shifts in demand, and so guide the interbank interest rate.

There were several features of the Chinese banking system in the 2000s that complicated this neat theoretical picture. First, the exchange rate peg forced the PBC to purchase foreign exchange with domestic currency as the market required. There was already a structural reserve surplus at the beginning of the decade, and mounting current account surpluses forced the central bank to continue feeding large quantities of reserves into the system. In Sun's (2015 [2004], p. 46) terminology, there was a large 'spontaneous' element to China's reserve supply, which policy struggled to fully offset. Second, many Chinese banks were not the optimisers presumed by the theory. They were often content to passively allow their buffer stocks of excess reserves to fluctuate, rather than actively managing them. This left these banks with large spare capacity for expansion, and made interbank market demand somewhat unpredictable, complicating policy control of rates. Further, because other banks were more active in engaging with the interbank market, and worked with much lower excess reserves, it was difficult for the central bank to drain reserves from the more-liquid banks without causing rates to spike and causing problems for the less liquid.

All this meant that the PBC could not be confident either of its control of interbank market conditions or of the influence of these conditions on bank lending. After policy turned towards restraint from late 2002, credit growth continued to far outpace the target. It was clear that direct banking controls of various kinds would remain absolutely necessary to a workable monetary policy for the foreseeable future: especially the variable required reserve ratio and window guidance.

For a while, the PBC attempted to sterilise the impact of foreign exchange inflows on the monetary base mainly with the use of a new market instrument, central bank bills. But the Bank found it difficult to sell these in sufficient quantities at acceptable yields, and turned to a control measure to 'deeply freeze' liquidity: adjustments in the required reserve ratio. This allowed policymakers to lock away large quantities of reserves at will, leaving open market operations to do the finer work of smoothing and directing interest rates. But even with required reserve adjustments isolating the monetary base from foreign exchange inflow, the PBC did not have the firm or fine control of interbank rates typically enjoyed by many central banks elsewhere. It attempted to smooth rates and guide them, but did not claim any ability to set them.

The central bank did, however, have substantial direct control over bank interest rates. The deposit rate ceiling and loan rate floor remained in place throughout this period. The former was binding, in the sense that actual deposit rates tended to be at the ceilings, so that they moved when the ceiling moved. Loan rates, on the other hand, were generally above the floor, so official control was not as tight. In practice, however, actual loan rates tended to move with official benchmarks. These were generally not market-clearing rates; banks tended to ration credit at administratively set rates. If demand for bank credit had been sensitive to loan rates, direct control over these would have given authorities a simple and reliable transmission mechanism. But borrowers were generally not sensitive to the rates at which they borrowed, at least not within the range of rates experienced. A substantial increase in bank interest rates was a part of policy tightening from 2006, but policymakers could not rely upon it to restrain credit growth.

In spite of the PBCs efforts in draining liquidity, the banking system still had too much unused lending capacity. Policy therefore continued to depend on directly controlling bank credit through its 'window guidance' directives. These were a lynchpin of restraint between 2003 and 2008. Window guidance was loosened somewhat around mid-decade, but leaned on heavily again from 2006—backed by penalty 'special bills' issued mandatorily to banks that did not comply, and supported by the revival of an old 75% loan-to-deposit cap.

Reliance on direct bank controls were not simply a vestige of an older, more statist policy regime, to be gradually abandoned with the transition to 'normalised' monetary policy based on the international macroeconomic consensus. Adopting a 'normal' policy commitment to controlling inflation was incompatible with reliance on 'normal' market-based policy in Chinese conditions. The former commitment led policy in the 2000s to rely *increasingly* on direct controls once it needed to restrain credit growth. Direct controls were also not an alternative to market-based policy in China, but a precondition for them. Given the exchange rate peg, Chinese authorities needed the blunt instrument of the variable required reserve ratio to insulate the interbank market from the monetary consequences of foreign exchange inflow, in order to make market-based policy even thinkable. Even if the exchange rate had been left to float, it is doubtful that the interbank market would have been ready to be the main venue for monetary policy in China. Standard monetary policy theory tends to take for granted the existence of a deep interbank market, and the fact that banks are responsive to conditions on that market in managing their balance sheets. Neither of these things were yet the case in China in the 2000s. The interbank market grew enormously over the decade, and became more important to the banking system, but it was not yet able to function as a fulcrum for monetary policy.

8.2 Into the 2010s

Limits to bank-centred policy could be seen before 2008. As direct restraint on bank lending strengthened, other forms of financing to the non-financial private sector grew rapidly, as can be seen in Fig. 2.1. From 2006 to 2008, strong bank loan growth was accompanied by very rapid growth in other forms of financing to non-financial enterprises and households. Bond and equity issuance both showed major growth, as did other forms of non-loan finance. Banks were in fact highly involved in these other financial channels. They held bonds directly—increasingly including private bonds. Since window guidance focused on restricting loans, it encouraged banks to hold 'investment' assets on their books instead. Banks did not invest in equities directly, but were a major source of finance to institutional investors purchasing new issues (Walter and Howie 2012, p. 31).

The other forms would later be referred to as a Chinese variant of 'shadow banking', and commercial banks were involved in all these channels in one way or another (Dang et al. 2014; Li et al. 2014; Elliott et al. 2015; Sheng and Soon 2015; Tsai 2015; Li 2016; Collier 2017; Gabor 2018). The most important components of the 'other' category 2006–2008 were trust loans, bankers' acceptances, and entrusted loans. Trust loans were simply loans made by trust companies, a form of non-bank financial institution. Bankers' acceptances generally provided short-term commercial credit, with the bank issuing a paper guarantee of a payment on some date in the future, in return for the borrower's own promise to pay. A firm could use the acceptance to pay for goods from a supplier, who could then sell the paper at a discount if they needed money before maturity. This effectively created a form of off-balance sheet bank credit and a quasi-money instrument (Elliott et al. 2015, p. 7).

Entrusted loans are loans made between firms, but under the auspices of a bank. The bank acts as an agent between its customers: The lending firm bears the risk and receives the interest, less a fee paid to the bank. They originated after a 1996 regulation prohibited direct inter-firm lending, and grew rapidly from 2004. Their rise had much to do with the build-up of spare deposits on non-financial firm books (see Table 2.3), as well as the uneven distribution of these spare deposits and of access to bank credit. Put simply, some firms—particularly state-owned firms—had both plenty of spare money and access to bank loans, while others—particularly private firms—had neither. The interest rate on entrusted loans had a premium of around 2 percentage points on bank loans, so firms with access to credit could profitably borrow from banks and lend it on in this way (Collier 2017, pp. 93–94). This enabled arbitrage around window guidance requests: Banks could be prevented from lending directly to certain sectors, and yet arrange entrusted loans either from firms' idle deposits, or from the proceeds of new loans to firms. Banks could even bring entrusted loans on balance sheet by purchasing the beneficiary rights—effectively purchasing the loan from the original lending firm, though it would appear as an 'investment' rather than a 'loan' on the bank's balance sheet, circumventing loan restrictions (Chen et al. 2016).

There were only a few scattered mentions of these financing channels in PBC monetary policy reports before the end of 2008. They were not yet discussed as a problem for policy control, but often as welcome channels for finance to enterprises underserved by the banks. For example, bankers' acceptances were described as 'an important channel for [small and medium-sized enterprises] to obtain financial support, enhance their payment ability, and ensure normal business operations' (PBC 2008a, p. 5). Trusts were described as institutions to be regulated and fostered to diversify the financial system, with their 'wealth management and other products... to facilitate the scientific development of trust investment companies and to protect the legitimate interests of the investors' (PBC 2007, p. 19).

Only from 2011 did the central bank present 'aggregate financing' data combining bank loans with other sources of finance, though this was calculated back to 2002 (as presented here in Fig. 2.1). By that point, the financial landscape had been reshaped by the enormous post-2008 stimulus package (Tsai 2015; Collier 2017, pp. 25–33), combined with expansionary monetary policy until mid-2010. The fiscal and monetary stimulus had two main impacts on non-loan finance: the growth of local governments as a financial nexus, and the rise of bank and trust 'wealth management products'.

The fiscal stimulus package was originally announced in November 2008 as 4 trillion RMB of new expenditure (US$586 billion)—already much larger relative to GDP than the United States stimulus package of 2009—and would ultimately expand to 12 trillion RMB (Tsai 2015, p. 70). But less than a third of this was to be provided from the central government budget—the rest was left to lower levels of government to raise. Restrictions on local government direct borrowing meant this was channelled through thousands of 'local government financing vehicles', which 'sprang up to broker off balance sheet loans between state banks and local governments that offered revenues from land sales and real estate as collateral' (Tsai 2015, p. 70; and see Collier 2017, pp. 53–72). Window guidance and abundant interbank market liquidity encouraged the large state-owned banks to lend liberally until mid-2010. This had an unforeseen effect in intensifying competition for deposits: With the 75% loan-to-deposit cap still in place, banks needed to retain enough deposits to support their expansion. The deposit rate cap continued to block competition on price, but banks used gifts and other inducements, and the large state-owned banks with their far-reaching networks were at an advantage in retaining deposits. Smaller banks turned to other measures: especially 'wealth management products' (Acharya et al. 2017). These packaged returns from a pool of underlying investments, somewhat like securitisation, and were sold as high-yield substitutes for deposits. Risks legally remained with the investor, but investors often presumed that banks guaranteed both returns and principal (Elliott et al. 2015, p. 2). Banks drew fees from managing these products (and often invested directly in them themselves [Collier 2017, p. 113–114]), but they were not otherwise on the balance sheet.

Once monetary policy turned back towards restraint after 2010, Chinese 'shadow banking' came into its own as a way around window guidance and other direct bank controls. Wealth management products continued to grow rapidly, directly in response to the tightening, as an off-balance sheet channel for both banks and trusts—often working together to circumvent rules preventing an institution from funding its own loans in this way (Funke et al. 2015, pp. 7–11). Bank loans continued to shrink as a proportion of aggregate financing to firms and households. In 2013 they (including foreign currency loans) made up just 55% of net new finance. Entrusted loans, trust loans, and bankers' acceptances together made up 30%, with much of the rest comprised of bond issuance (10%). Equities were a much more minor source of finance than they had been in 2006–2007, at just 1%, while there was a 4% unidentified residual.[1] Wealth management products do not appear in this data because the aggregate financing statistics record the form in which the finance reaches the borrower, not the form in which it was raised: The

[1]This data is from the PBC/CEIC 'Aggregate financing' series.

products would have channelled funds into these categories, presumably mainly trust loans and bonds.

This made for a plausible story that financial innovation was routing around bank controls and forcing a shift towards a market-based system in spite of authorities. But as Gabor (2018) argues, things have proven more complicated. Chinese authorities proved willing and able to combine tighter restrictions on some financing activity with legitimate—and regulated—channels for others. 'Indeed, events since 2014 suggest that we should not simply read Chinese shadow banking as an elaborate artifice of regulatory arbitrage, but rather as a gradual policy experiment with liberalising the financial sector by encouraging securities markets' (Gabor 2018, p. 401).

Even as authorities were deregulating bank deposit rates and lifting the 75% loan-to-deposit ratio, they were imposing new restraints on entrusted loans, wealth management products and other 'shadow banking' instruments. Around the same time, local governments were permitted to issue bonds, allowing for an alternative to the labyrinthine local government financing vehicles. In 2017, wealth management products were brought onto bank balance sheets, where they became subject to bank prudential regulation (Gabor 2018, p. 402). 2013 turned out to be low-tide for bank lending as a proportion of aggregate financing: By 2015 the bank loan share of net new financing was 69%. In 2018 it was 79%, with entrusted loan, trust loan and bankers' acceptance bill finance shrinking. Most of the remainder was bond finance—corporate and municipal,[2] though this was now joined by a substantial component of asset-backed securities—a larger source than equity issuance—as well as a large unidentified 'other'.

This is not to say that Chinese policymakers had regained control of the financial system. The interplay between regulation and financial innovation continued much as it has elsewhere: One practice is suppressed only for new devices to spring up elsewhere. Acharya et al. (2017, pp. 8–9) write of the 'dynamic game' between regulators and financial institutions in China, while Gabor suggests that China has been moving from its older bank-based form of 'shadow banking' to a new form based more directly in repo and securities markets—and indeed, turnover in the repo market is now many times bigger than it was in the 2000s (Gabor 2018, pp. 401–406).

[2] Data is again from the PBC/CEIC 'Aggregate financing' series. The PBC has decided to include local government bond financing as part of 'aggregate financing', unlike central government bond issuance.

Chinese policy has certainly continued to develop policy focused on interest rates in the interbank market. The framework now combines daily open market operations in the repo market with a standing lending facility whereby banks can access medium-term funding from the central bank. The rate on this funding now sets an upper bound to medium-term interbank rates, while the rate paid on excess reserves continues to set a floor: a rate 'corridor' with both bounds under policy control (Chen et al. 2017, p. 5). At the same time, Chinese monetary policy has not abandoned the direct controls we described in earlier chapters. Bank interest rates have been formally liberalised, but banks still tend to follow official benchmarks in practice for both lending (Chen et al. 2017, p. 5) and deposits. In 2018, policymakers were still talking about interest rate liberalisation as an ongoing project, now involving weaning the banks from official guidance (Bi et al. 2018). Required reserve ratios have been lowered periodically since 2011, and never raised, but they remain an instrument.[3] A series of cuts in 2018–2019 have played a part in the turn to looser policy, and there is nothing to stop a reversal when policy turns back to restraint. Window guidance likewise remains a regular instrument of policy. Banks remain at the centre of the Chinese financial system; the large state-owned banks remain dominant; and direct controls remain potent. In China, monetary policy continues to involve a combination of controls and market-based policy; it cannot be taken for granted that the former will supplant the latter. The experience of tightening in the 2000s tells us that we should not extrapolate too far from what happens in times of policy easing in any case: The direct controls remain in reserve to be used in the time of need.

References

Acharya, Viral V., Jun Qian, and Zhishu Yang. 2017. "In the shadow of banks: Wealth management products and issuing banks' risk in China." Unpublished paper. Available at https://jrc.princeton.edu/sites/jrc/files/qian_jun-shadowbank-china-aqy-10feb17-all.pdf. 17 May 2019.

Bi, Xiaowen, Li Zheng, Shu Zhang, and Ryan Woo. 2018. "China's central bank to relax commercial banks' deposit rate ceiling: Sources." *Reuters*, 13 April. Available at https://www.reuters.com/article/us-china-cenbank-deposits/

[3] Data from PBC/CEIC: 'Required reserve ratio'.

chinas-central-bank-to-relax-commercial-banks-deposit-rate-ceiling-sources-idUSKBN1HK0T3. 15 May 2019.

Burdekin, Richard C. K., and Pierre L. Siklos. 2008. "What has driven Chinese monetary policy since 1990? Investigating the People's Bank's policy rule." *Journal of International Money and Finance* 27, pp. 847–859.

Chen, Hongyi, Michael Funke, Ivan Lozev, and Andrew Tsang. 2017. "To guide or not to guide? Quantitative monetary policy tools and macroeconomic dynamics in China." Bank of Finland Institute for Economies in Transition Discussion Papers 3.

Chen, Kaiji, Jue Ren, and Tao Zha. 2016. "What we learn from China's rising shadow banking: Exploring the nexus of monetary tightening and banks' role in entrusted lending." NBER Working Paper Series 21890.

Collier, Andrew. 2017. *Shadow banking and the rise of capitalism in China.* Singapore: Palgrave Macmillan.

Dang, Tri Vi, Honglin Wang, and Aidan Yao. 2014. "Chinese shadow banking: Bank-centric misperceptions." Hong Kong Institute for Monetary Research Working Paper 22.

Elliott, Douglas, Arthur Kroeber, and Yu Qiao. 2015. "Shadow banking in China: A primer." Economic Studies at Brookings. Available at https://www.brookings.edu/wp-content/uploads/2016/06/shadow_banking_china_elliott_kroeber_yu.pdf. 13 May 2019.

Funke, Michael, Petar Mihaylovski, and Haibin Zhu. 2015. "Monetary policy transmission in China: A DSGE model with parallel shadow banking and interest rate control." Bank of Finland Institute for Economies in Transition Discussion Paper 9.

Gabor, Daniela. 2018. "Goodbye (Chinese) shadow banking, hello market-based finance." *Development and Change* 49 (2), pp. 394–419.

Gerlach, Stefan, and Janet Kong. 2005. "Money and inflation in China." Hong Kong Monetary Authority Research Memorandum 04/2005.

Goodhart, Charles A. E. 1989. *Money, information, and uncertainty.* Houndmills: Macmillan.

Li, Cindy. 2016. "The changing face of shadow banking in China." *Federal Reserve Bank of San Francisco Asia Focus*, December, pp. 1–8.

Li, Jianjun, Sara Hsu, and Yanzhi Qin. 2014. "Shadow banking in China: Institutional risks." *China Economic Review* 31, pp. 119–129.

People's Bank of China. 2007. *Monetary Policy Report, Quarter 1.* Beijing: People's Bank of China.

People's Bank of China. 2008a. *Monetary Policy Report, Quarter 2.* Beijing: People's Bank of China.

People's Bank of China. 2008b. *Monetary Policy Report, Quarter 4.* Beijing: People's Bank of China.

Sheng, Andrew, and Ng Chow Soon (eds.). 2015. *Bringing shadow banking into the light: Opportunity for financial reform in China*. Hong Kong: Fung Global Institute.

Sun, Guofeng. 2015. *Reforms in China's monetary policy: A frontbencher's perspective*. New York: Palgrave Macmillan.

Tsai, Kellee S. 2015. "The political economy of state capitalism and shadow banking in China." *Issues & Studies* 51 (1), pp. 55–97.

Walter, Carl E., and Fraser J. T. Howie. 2012. *Red capitalism: The fragile financial foundation of China's extraordinary rise*, 2nd ed. Singapore: Wiley.

References

Acharya, Viral V., Jun Qian, and Zhishu Yang. 2017. "In the shadow of banks: Wealth management products and issuing banks' risk in China." Unpublished paper. Available at https://jrc.princeton.edu/sites/jrc/files/qian_jun-shadowbank-china-aqy-10feb17-all.pdf. 17 May 2019.

Allen, Franklin, Xian Gu, and Jun Qian. 2018. "The People's Bank of China: From 1948 to 2016." In Rodney Edvinsson, Tor Jacobcon, and Daniel Waldenstrom (eds.). *Sveriges Riksbank and the history of central banking*, pp. 418–453. Cambridge: Cambridge University Press.

Angrick, Stefan, and Naoyuki Yoshino. 2018. "From window guidance to interbank rates: Tracing the transition of monetary policy in Japan and China." Bank of Finland Institute for Economies in Transition Discussion Papers 4.

Arestis, Philip. 2007. "What is the new consensus in macroeconomics?" In Philip Arestis (ed.). *Is there a new consensus in macroeconomics?*, pp. 22–42. London: Palgrave Macmillan.

Arestis, Philip, and Malcolm Sawyer. 2008. "A critical reconsideration of the foundations of monetary policy in the new consensus macroeconomics framework." *Cambridge Journal of Economics* 32 (5), pp. 761–779.

Baharumshah, Ahmad Zubaidi, Siti Hamizah Mohd, and Marial Awou Yol. 2009. "Stock prices and demand for money in China: New evidence." *Journal of International Financial Markets, Institutions and Money* 19, pp. 171–187.

Bahmani-Oskooee, Mohsen, and Yongqing Wang. 2007. "How stable is the demand for money in China?" *Journal of Economic Development* 32, pp. 21–33.

M. Beggs and L. Deer, *Remaking Monetary Policy in China*,
https://doi.org/10.1007/978-981-13-9726-4

Bai, Chong-En, Chang-Tai Hsieh, and Yingyi Qian. 2006. "The return to capital in China." NBER Working Paper Series 12755.

Beggs, Michael. 2015. *Inflation and the making of Australian macroeconomic policy, 1945–85*. Houndmills: Palgrave Macmillan.

Bell, Stephen, and Hui Feng. 2013. *The rise of the People's Bank of China: The politics of institutional change*. Cambridge, MA: Harvard University Press.

Bernanke, Ben S., and Alan S. Blinder. 1992. "The federal funds rate and the channels of monetary transmission." *American Economic Review* 82 (4), pp. 901–921.

Bernanke, Ben S., and Ilian Mihov. 1998. "The liquidity effect and long-run neutrality." NBER Working Paper 6608.

Bernanke, Ben S., and Mark Gertler. 1995. "Inside the black box: The credit channel of monetary policy transmission." *Journal of Economic Perspectives* 9 (4), pp. 27–48.

Bi, Xiaowen, Li Zheng, Shu Zhang, and Ryan Woo. 2018. "China's central bank to relax commercial banks' deposit rate ceiling: Sources." *Reuters*, 13 April. Available at https://www.reuters.com/article/us-china-cenbank-deposits/chinas-central-bank-to-relax-commercial-banks-deposit-rate-ceiling-sources-idUSKBN1HK0T3. 15 May 2019.

Blinder, Alan S. 1998. *Central banking in theory and practice*. Cambridge, MA: MIT Press.

Bofinger, Peter. 2001. *Monetary policy: Goals, institutions, strategies, and instruments*. Oxford: Oxford University Press.

Burdekin, Richard C. K., and Pierre L. Siklos. 2008. "What has driven Chinese monetary policy since 1990? Investigating the People's Bank's policy rule." *Journal of International Money and Finance* 27, pp. 847–859.

Burger, Albert E., and Robert H. Rasche. 1977. "Revision of the monetary base." *Federal Reserve Bank of St Louis Review*, July, pp. 13–28.

Cao, Honghui, and Mengmeng Ma. 2007. "The stock exchange market." In Yang Li (ed.). *China's banking & financial markets: The internal research report of the Chinese government*, pp. 223–248. Singapore: Wiley.

Cao, Yujin, Jidong Chen, and Qinghua Zhang. 2018. "Housing investment in Urban China." *Journal of Comparative Economics* 46, pp. 212–247.

CEIC China Premium Database. https://www.ceicdata.com/.

Chen, Baizhu. 1997. "Long-run money demand and inflation in China." *Journal of Macroeconomics* 19 (3), pp. 609–617.

Chen, Hongyi, Qianying Chen, and Stefan Gerlach. 2013. "The implementation of monetary policy in China: The interbank market and bank lending." In Bang Nam Jeon and María Pía Olivero (eds.). *Global banking, financial markets and crises*, pp. 31–69. Bingley: Emerald Group Publishing.

Chen, Hongyi, Michael Funke, Ivan Lozev, and Andrew Tsang. 2017. "To guide or not to guide? Quantitative monetary policy tools and macroeconomic dynamics in China." Bank of Finland Institute for Economies in Transition Discussion Papers 3.

Chen, Kaiji, Jue Ren, and Tao Zha. 2016. "What we learn from China's rising shadow banking: Exploring the nexus of monetary tightening and banks' role in entrusted lending." NBER Working Paper Series 21890.

Chick, Victoria. 1983. *Macroeconomics after Keynes : A reconsideration of the general theory*. Cambridge: MIT Press.

Chick, Victoria, and Sheila Dow. 2002. "Monetary policy with endogenous money and liquidity preference: A nondualistic treatment." *Journal of Post Keynesian Economics* 24 (4), pp. 587–607.

Collier, Andrew. 2017. *Shadow banking and the rise of capitalism in China*. Singapore: Palgrave Macmillan.

Dang, Tri Vi, Honglin Wang, and Aidan Yao. 2014. "Chinese shadow banking: Bank-centric misperceptions." Hong Kong Institute for Monetary Research Working Paper 22.

Delatte, Anne-Laure. 2008. "Monetary policy and macrocontrol in China: The actual impact of window guidance." Unpublished paper. Available at http://citeseerx.ist.psu.edu/viewdoc/download?doi=10.1.1.651.7744&rep=rep1&type=pdf. 15 April 2019.

Deng, Haiqing, and Xi Chen. 2016. *Reforging the Central Bank: The top-level design of the Chinese financial system in the new normal*. Singapore: World Scientific Publishing.

Elliott, Douglas, Arthur Kroeber, and Yu Qiao. 2015. "Shadow banking in China: A primer." Economic Studies at Brookings. Available at https://www.brookings.edu/wp-content/uploads/2016/06/shadow_banking_china_elliott_kroeber_yu.pdf. 13 May 2019.

Feinman, Joshua. 1993. "Estimating the open market desk's daily reaction function." *Journal of Money, Credit and Banking* 25 (2), pp. 231–247.

Feyzioglu, Tarhan, Nathan Porter, and Elod Takats. 2009. "Interest rate liberalisation in China." IMF Working Papers 09/171.

Forssbaeck, Jens, and Lars Oxelheim. 2007. "The transition to market-based monetary policy: What can China learn from the European experience?" *Journal of Asian Economics* 18, pp. 257–283.

Freixas, Xavier, and Jean-Charles Rochet. 2008. *Microeconomics of banking*. Cambridge, MA: MIT Press.

Funke, Michael, Petar Mihaylovski, and Haibin Zhu. 2015. "Monetary policy transmission in China: A DSGE model with parallel shadow banking and interest rate control." Bank of Finland Institute for Economies in Transition Discussion Paper 9.

Gabor, Daniela. 2018. "Goodbye (Chinese) shadow banking, hello market-based finance." *Development and Change* 49 (2), pp. 394–419.

Gabor, Tamas. 2012. "China's monetary sterilisation and its economical relationship with the European Union." *Crisis Aftermath: Economic policy changes in the EU and its member states*. International Conference Proceedings, pp. 356–381. Available at https://ssrn.com/abstract=2159944. 16 April 2019.

Gao, Zhanjun. 2007. "The inter-bank bond market." In Yang Li (ed.). *China's banking & financial markets: The internal research report of the Chinese government*, pp. 191–222. Singapore: Wiley.

Geiger, Michael. 2008. "Instruments of monetary policy in China and their effectiveness: 1994–2006." UNCTAD Discussion Paper 2008 (2).

Geiger, Michael. 2010. *Monetary policy in China: Institutions, targets, instruments and strategies*. Dissertation, Bayerischen Julius-Maximillians-Universistat Wurzburg.

Gerlach, Stefan, and Janet Kong. 2005. "Money and inflation in China." Hong Kong Monetary Authority Research Memorandum 04/2005.

Girardin, Eric. 1997. *Banking sector reform and credit control in China*. Paris: OECD Development Centre.

Girardin, Eric, Sandrine Lunven, and Guonan Ma. 2017. "China's evolving monetary policy rule: From inflation-accommodating to anti-inflation policy." Bank for International Settlements Working Papers 641.

Glaeser, Edward, Wei Huang, Yueran Ma, and Andrei Shleifer. 2017. "A real estate boom with Chinese characteristics." *Journal of Economic Perspectives* 31 (1), pp. 93–116.

Godley, Wynne, and Marc Lavoie. 2007. *Monetary economics: An integrated approach the credit, money, income, production and wealth*. Houndmills: Palgrave Macmillan.

Goodhart, Charles A. E. 1989. *Money, information, and uncertainty*. Houndmills: Macmillan.

Goodhart, Charles A. E. 2007. "Whatever became of the monetary aggregates?" *National Institute Economic Review* 200, pp. 56–61.

Green, Stephen. 2005. "Making monetary policy work in China: A report from the money market front line." Stanford Center for International Development Working Paper 245.

Guo, Xiaoting. 2007. "The securities industry." In Yang Li (ed.). *China's banking & financial markets: The internal research report of the Chinese government*, pp. 133–158. Singapore: Wiley.

Hachem, Kinda Cheryl, and Zheng Michael Song. 2017. "Liquidity regulation and credit booms: Theory and evidence from China." NBER Working Paper Series 21880.

Hafer, Rik W., and Ali M. Kutan. 1994. "Economic reforms and long-run money demand in China: Implications for monetary policy." *Southern Economic Journal* 60 (4), pp. 936–945.

Hamilton, James D. 1997. "Measuring the liquidity effect." *American Economic Review* 87 (1), pp. 80–97.

Hamilton, James D. 1998. "The supply and demand for Federal Reserve deposits." *Carnegie-Rochester Conference Series on Public Policy* 49 (1), pp. 45–52.

He, Dong, and Honglin Wang. 2011. "Dual-track interest rates and the conduct of monetary policy in China." Hong Kong Institute for Monetary Research Working Paper 21.

He, Dong, and Honglin Wang. 2012. "Dual-track interest rates and the conduct of monetary policy in China." *China Economic Review* 23, 928–947.

He, Dong, Honglin Wang, and Xiangrong Yu. 2015. "Interest rate determination in China: Past, present, and future." *International Journal of Central Banking* 11 (4), pp. 255–277.

Huang, Guobo. 1994. "Money demand in China in the reform period: An error correction model." *Applied Economics* 26, pp. 713–719.

International Monetary Fund. 2000. *Monetary and financial statistics manual.* Washington, DC: International Monetary Fund.

Kalecki, Michal. 1965. *Theory of economic dynamics.* London: Unwin University Books.

Koivu, Tuuli. 2009. "Has the Chinese economy become more sensitive to interest rates? Studying credit demand in China." *China Economic Review* 20 (3), pp. 455–470.

Kothari, S. P., Jonathan Lewellen, and Jerold B. Warner. 2014. "The behaviour of aggregate corporate investment." MIT Sloan School Working Papers 5112-14.

Lardy, Nicholas R. 2008. "Financial repression in China." Peterson Institute Policy Brief PB08.

Laurens, Bernard J., and Rodolfo Maino. 2007. "China: Strengthening monetary policy implementation." IMF Working Paper 07/14.

Lavoie, Marc, and Peng Wang. 2012. "The 'compensation' thesis, as exemplified by the case of the Chinese central bank." *International Review of Applied Economics* 26 (3), pp. 287–301.

Li, Cindy. 2016. "The changing face of shadow banking in China." *Federal Reserve Bank of San Francisco Asia Focus*, December, pp. 1–8.

Li, Jianjun, Sara Hsu, and Yanzhi Qin. 2014. "Shadow banking in China: Institutional risks." *China Economic Review* 31, pp. 119–129.

Li, Qing, Weiqiang Ye, and Yuqing Feng. 2007. Cures for China's feverish stock market. *Caijing English Newsletter*, 11 June.

Li, Yang, and Xingyun Peng. 2002. "The money market in China: Theory and practice." *China & World Economy* 3, pp. 3–10.

Liu, Zheng, Pengfei Wang, and Zhiwei Xu. 2017. "Interest-rate liberalisation and capital misallocations." Federal Reserve Bank of San Francisco Working Paper 2017-15.

Ma, Guonan, Yan Xiandong, and Liu Xi. 2011. "China's evolving reserve requirements." BIS Working Papers 360.

Mehrling, Perry. 2011. *The New Lombard Street: How the Fed became the dealer of last resort.* Princeton: Princeton University Press.

Mehrotra, Aaron. 2007. "Exchange and interest rate channels during a deflationary era: Evidence from Japan, Hong Kong and China." *Journal of Comparative Economics* 35 (1), pp. 188–210.

Mehrotra, Aaron. 2008. "Demand for money in transition: Evidence from China's disinflation." *International Advances in Economic Research* 14, 36–47.

Meulendyke, Ann-Marie. 1998. *US monetary policy and financial markets.* New York: Federal Reserve Bank of New York.

Michell, Jo. 2012. *Credit and investment in China: A flow-of-funds analysis.* PhD thesis, SOAS, University of London.

Mishkin, Frederic S. 1995. *Economics of money, banking, and financial markets*, 4th ed. New York: HarperCollins.

Mishkin, Frederic S. 2004. *Economics of money, banking, and financial markets*, 7th ed. Boston: Addison Wesley.

Naughton, Barry. 2007. *The Chinese economy: Transitions and growth.* Cambridge, MA: MIT Press.

OECD. 2019. "Household financial assets (indicator)." Available at https://doi.org/10.1787/7519b9dc-en. 3 April 2019.

People's Bank of China. 2003a. *Monetary Policy Report, Quarter 3.* Beijing: People's Bank of China.

People's Bank of China. 2003b. *Monetary Policy Report, Quarter 4.* Beijing: People's Bank of China.

People's Bank of China. 2004. *Monetary Policy Report, Quarter 1.* Beijing: People's Bank of China.

People's Bank of China. 2005a. *Monetary Policy Report, Quarter 1.* Beijing: People's Bank of China.

People's Bank of China. 2005b. *Monetary Policy Report, Quarter 2.* Beijing: People's Bank of China.

People's Bank of China. 2005c. *Monetary Policy Report, Quarter 3.* Beijing: People's Bank of China.

People's Bank of China. 2005d. *Monetary Policy Report, Quarter 4.* Beijing: People's Bank of China.

People's Bank of China. 2006a. *Monetary Policy Report, Quarter 1.* Beijing: People's Bank of China.

People's Bank of China. 2006b. *Monetary Policy Report, Quarter 2.* Beijing: People's Bank of China.

People's Bank of China. 2006c. *Monetary Policy Report, Quarter 3.* Beijing: People's Bank of China.

People's Bank of China. 2006d. *Monetary Policy Report, Quarter 4.* Beijing: People's Bank of China.

People's Bank of China. 2007a. *Monetary Policy Report, Quarter 1.* Beijing: People's Bank of China.

People's Bank of China. 2007b. *Monetary Policy Report, Quarter 2*. Beijing: People's Bank of China.

People's Bank of China. 2007c. *Monetary Policy Report, Quarter 3*. Beijing: People's Bank of China.

People's Bank of China. 2007d. *Monetary Policy Report, Quarter 4*. Beijing: People's Bank of China.

People's Bank of China. 2008a. *Monetary Policy Report, Quarter 1*. Beijing: People's Bank of China.

People's Bank of China. 2008b. *Monetary Policy Report, Quarter 2*. Beijing: People's Bank of China.

People's Bank of China. 2008c. *Monetary Policy Report, Quarter 4*. Beijing: People's Bank of China.

People's Bank of China. 2011. *Monetary Policy Report, Quarter 1*. Beijing: People's Bank of China.

People's Bank of China. 2015. *Monetary Policy Report, Quarter 3*. Beijing: People's Bank of China.

Poole, William. 1970. "Optimal choice of monetary policy instruments in a simple stochastic monetary model." *Quarterly Journal of Economics* 84, pp. 197–216.

Porter, Nathan, and TengTeng Xu. 2009. "What drives China's interbank market?" IMF Working Paper 09/189.

Porter, Nathan, and TengTeng Xu. 2016. "Money-market rates and retail interest regulation in China: The disconnect between interbank and retail credit conditions." *International Journal of Central Banking* 12 (1), pp. 143–198.

Prasad, Eswar. 2008. "Monetary policy independence, the currency regime, and the capital account in China." In Morris Goldstein and Nicholas R. Lardy (eds.). *Debating China's exchange rate policy*, pp. 77–92. Washington, DC: Peterson Institute for International Economics.

Sheng, Andrew and Ng Chow Soon (eds.). 2015. *Bringing shadow banking into the light: Opportunity for financial reform in China*. Hong Kong: Fung Global Institute.

Shevlin, Aidan. 2017. "An expanded tool kit for the People's Bank of China." J. P. Morgan. Available at https://blog.jpmorganinstitutional.com/2017/05/expanded-tool-kit-peoples-bank-china. 2 April 2019.

Shu, Chang, and Brian Ng. 2010. "Monetary stance and policy objectives in China." *Hong Kong Monetary Authority China Economic Issues* 1/10.

Stigum, Marcia, and Anthony Crescenzi. 2007. *Stigum's money market*. New York: McGraw-Hill.

Strongin, Steven. 1995. "The identification of monetary policy disturbances explaining the liquidity puzzle." *Journal of Monetary Economics* 35, pp. 463–497.

Sun, Guofeng. 2015. *Reforms in China's monetary policy: A frontbencher's perspective*. New York: Palgrave Macmillan.

Sun, Rongrong. 2013. "Does monetary policy matter in China? A narrative approach." *China Economic Review* 26, pp. 56–74.

Toporowski, Jan. 2008. "Excess capital and liquidity management." Levy Economics Institute Working Paper 549.

Tsai, Kellee S. 2002. *Back-Alley banking: Private entrepreneurs in China*. Ithaca, NY: Cornell University Press.

Tsai, Kellee S. 2015. "The political economy of state capitalism and shadow banking in China." *Issues & Studies* 51 (1), pp. 55–97.

Walter, Carl E., and Fraser J. T. Howie. 2012. *Red capitalism: The fragile financial foundation of China's extraordinary rise*, 2 ed. Singapore: Wiley.

Wang, Gang, and Zhuqing Mao. 2016. "Annual developments in banking regulation." In Bin Hu, Zhentao Yin, and Liansheng Zheng (eds.). *Development of China's financial supervision and regulation*, pp. 59–100. New York: Palgrave Macmillan.

Wu, Ge. 2009. "Broad money demand and asset substitution in China." IMF Working Paper 09/131.

Xie, Ping. 2004. "China's monetary policy: 1998–2002." Stanford Center for International Development Working Paper 217.

Xiong, Weibo. 2012. "Measuring the monetary policy stance of the People's Bank of China: An ordered probit analysis." *China Economic Review* 23 (3), pp. 512–533.

Yan, Qingmin, and Jianhua Li. 2016. *Regulating China's shadow banks*. Milton Park: Routledge.

Yi, Gang. 2015. "On the removal of the deposit rate ceiling." Summary of Discussion, 27 October 2015. People's Bank of China. Available at http://www.pbc.gov.cn/english/130724/2969444/index.html. 2 April 2019.

Yin, Jianfeng. 2007. "The banking industry." In Yang Li (ed.). *China's banking & financial markets: The internal research report of the Chinese government*, pp. 161–190. Singapore: Wiley.

Yong, Cao. 2011. "The persistence of strong money supply growth in China: The forces of endogenous determinants." *Banks and Bank Systems* 6 (4), pp. 33–48.

Yu, Qiao, and Ping Xie. 1999. "Money aggregates management: Problems and prospects in China's economic transition." *Contemporary Economic Policy* 17 (1), pp. 33–43.

Zeng, Gang. 2007. "The banking industry." In Yang Li (ed.). *China's banking & financial markets: The internal research report of the Chinese government*, pp. 69–95. Singapore: Wiley.

Zuo, Haomiao, and Sung Y. Park. 2011. "Money demand in China and time-varying cointegration." *China Economic Journal* 22 (3), pp. 330–343.

Index

A

Administered rates, 76, 79, 83, 87
Aggregate financing, 4, 10, 11, 109–111
Asian financial crisis, 3, 6, 19, 34, 68, 78, 85

B

Bank-centred policy, 108
Bank-control-based policy framework, 2
Bank deposits, 12, 21–23, 36, 37, 39, 48, 54, 68, 74, 79, 83, 103, 111
Bank interest rates, 41, 42, 95–97, 102, 106, 107, 112
Bank lending and deposit rates, 33, 78, 94
Bank liquidity preference, 32, 60, 105
Bank money multiplier approach, 31
Buffer stock, 43, 53, 55, 76, 84, 86, 104, 106
Buffer-stock demand for money, 52, 104

C

1995 Central Bank Law, 4
Chinese macroeconomic policy, 101
Chinese monetary policy, 1, 3, 47, 102, 112
Credit Plan, 5, 21, 26, 92
Currency stability, 4, 5

D

Dai Xianglong, 5
Deep freezing liquidity, 75, 106
Deflation, 68
Demand for deposits, 15, 16, 47, 51, 54, 55, 104, 105
Demand for money, 16, 22–24, 26, 47, 51, 52, 54, 55, 103, 104
Deposit and loan interest rates, 2, 33, 40, 55, 58, 79, 89, 97, 104

M. Beggs and L. Deer, *Remaking Monetary Policy in China*, https://doi.org/10.1007/978-981-13-9726-4

Direct bank controls, 3, 4, 107, 110
Direct banking controls, 2, 6, 56, 68, 96, 102, 106
Direct lending controls, 42
'Dual-track' interest rate regime, 33
'Dual-track' interest rate structure, 76

E
Excess reserves, 37, 42, 57–61, 76, 78, 83–87, 91, 94, 96, 97, 103, 105, 106, 112
Exchange rate peg, 68, 70, 73, 74, 104, 105, 107

F
Fiscal stimulus package, 102, 109
Flow-of-funds accounts, 13, 15, 52, 63
Foreign currency inflow, 68
Foreign exchange, 48, 49, 51, 55, 56, 59, 68, 69, 71, 72, 79, 87, 91, 104, 105
Foreign exchange inflow(s), 35, 72, 73, 79, 85, 90, 97, 106, 107
Foreign exchange purchases, 25, 59, 64, 68, 69, 71, 72, 75, 79, 84, 85, 89, 96, 97, 104
Foreign exchange sterilisation, 19

G
Global financial crisis, 6, 68, 95

H
Household demand for deposits, 13

I
Industrial organisation approach, 38, 40, 43, 47, 54, 60, 103, 104
Industrial organisation framework, 31, 38, 42, 46
Industrial organisation model, 40, 47, 51, 54, 80
Inflation, 4, 5, 24, 25, 68, 86, 91, 97, 103, 107
Interbank interest rates, 27, 43, 59, 60, 75–77, 84, 85, 88, 105
Interbank market instruments, 76, 87
Interbank market interest rates, 75, 84, 91
Interbank market rates, 62, 75, 76, 78, 83, 86, 87
Interbank markets, 2–4, 17, 18, 28, 32, 33, 40, 46, 51, 56–59, 61, 62, 68, 73, 76, 78–80, 85–88, 90–92, 97, 98, 102, 103, 105–107, 110, 112
Interbank money market, 32, 33
Interest rate liberalisation, 112
Interest rate targeting, 22

L
Lending controls, 4
Liquidity constraint, 46, 56
Liquidity management, 3, 6, 18, 19, 43, 58, 76, 90, 91
Liquidity surplus, 59, 62, 68

M
M2 targets, 21, 36
Market-based policy, 2, 3, 56, 62, 87, 89, 91, 92, 98, 105, 107, 112
Market instruments, 2, 3, 89, 106
Market interest rates, 5, 39, 42, 68, 73, 87, 89
Mishkin framework, 5
Mishkin textbook, 23, 27, 28
Monetary policy, 2–6, 16, 22, 23, 27, 40, 42, 45, 48, 58, 68, 71, 72,

91, 93, 94, 96, 102, 104, 106, 107, 109, 110, 112
Monetary policy transmission, 58
Monetary restraint, 25, 67
Monetary targeting, 22, 23, 25, 26, 103
Money multiplier, 23, 25, 26, 35–38, 43, 54, 60, 103
Money supply (M2), 9, 21, 23–25, 32–34, 36, 37, 47–51, 53, 56, 62, 64, 91, 97, 98, 103, 104
Money view, 32, 56

N
New consensus on monetary policy, 4
New macroeconomic consensus, 2, 5, 21, 27
'New normal', 2
Non-bank financial institutions, 17, 33, 40, 41, 51, 63, 78–80

O
Old normal, 3
Open market operations, 2–5, 42, 59, 69, 71, 72, 74–76, 79, 84–87, 89–91, 101, 106, 112

Q
Quantitative targets, 21–23, 103
Quantity targets, 25, 85

R
Repo market, 111, 112
Required reserve ratio, 37, 59, 73–75, 79, 85–87, 89, 95–97, 106, 107, 112
Reserve constraint, 28, 56
Reserve requirement, 2, 3, 5, 37, 42, 46, 56, 74, 75, 85, 90, 91, 95–97, 102
RRR adjustment, 75

S
Securities markets, 9, 111
Shadow banking, 3, 4, 102, 108, 110, 111
Sharemarket, 12, 13, 52
Sharemarket boom, 52, 88
Sterilisation, 26, 35, 69, 71, 73, 79, 85–87, 89, 90
Sterilising, 72, 84, 91, 96
Stockmarket, 88
Sun, Guofeng, 32, 37, 38, 45–47, 49, 56, 58, 60, 61, 68, 71–73, 84, 85, 104–106

T
Total social financing, 10
Transmission channels, 6, 27, 28
Transmission mechanism(s), 6, 23, 27, 28, 31, 32, 35, 91, 98, 107
Transmission processes of monetary policy, 21

U
US financial crisis, 101

W
Window guidance, 42, 92–98, 106–110, 112
Window guidance and credit quotas, 41

Y
Yi, Gang, 2

Z
Zhou, Xiaochuan, 6

The manufacturer's authorised representative in the EU is Springer Nature Customer Service Centre GmbH, Europaplatz 3, 69115 Heidelberg, Germany. If you have any concerns regarding our products, please contact ProductSafety@springernature.com

Printed and bound by CPI Group (UK) Ltd, Croydon, CR0 4YY
25/09/2026
02222897-0016